YORKSHIRE
MURDER CASEBOOK

STEVE FIELDING

COUNTRYSIDE BOOKS
NEWBURY · BERKSHIRE

First published 1997
© Steve Fielding 1997

COUNTRYSIDE BOOKS
3 Catherine Road
Newbury, Berkshire

ISBN 1 85306 490 4

Produced through MRM Associates Ltd., Reading
Typeset by Techniset Typesetters, Newton-le-Willows
Printed by J. W. Arrowsmith Ltd., Bristol

CONTENTS

INTRODUCTION

It was in London in the middle of the 18th century that Henry Fielding created the Bow Street Runners, the first attempt at an organised body of men specifically collected together to help fight a sharp increase in crime. Some 50 years later, in 1829, this ideal was taken a step further when the then Home Secretary, Sir Robert Peel, set up the Metropolitan Police Force, which we recognise now as the first police force. One of the most common types of crime the new law-enforcers were to fight was highway robbery. Probably the most famous of all highwaymen, Richard 'Dick' Turpin, has strong links with Yorkshire: in April 1739 he was hanged at York Castle.

In 1835, Parliament passed the Municipal Corporation Act, which empowered boroughs over a certain population to establish their own local police force. Among the first to do so was Leeds under the command of its first Chief Constable, William Heywood. Bradford soon followed suit, as did York, in creating a borough force.

As the Industrial Revolution gathered momentum during the 19th century, new aids to detection began to appear. By the turn of the century fingerprinting was starting to be recognised in the courtroom, and this was followed quickly by great strides in the fields of ballistics and in branches of forensics such as blood-grouping.

At first the bobbies on the beat had to rely on police whistles and the striking of truncheons on the kerb in a crude form of code to summon assistance, but later, radios were introduced. In 1911 the first mounted police appeared on the streets and when the motor car was invented, this too was soon utilised by the police force. Other significant advances in the police world were the training of a recognised pool of detectives and the formation of the CID; the acceptance of women police officers; the formation of the fire brigade, which was another task taken away from the overworked bobby; and the use of police dogs from the 1950s.

Yorkshire has a unique place in the annals of criminal history, since the county has supplied some of the most notorious murderers on record: John Haigh – the acid-bath murderer – was a Yorkshireman, as was John Reginald Halliday Christie – the notorious killer of

10 Rillington Place. Both these men committed their crimes away from the county, unlike Yorkshire Ripper Peter Sutcliffe, whose reign of terror horrified the whole nation in the late 1970s.

Yorkshire has also been the home to some infamous killers authorised by the State. Between 1883 and 1956, the latter days of capital punishment in Great Britain, more often than not the country's chief executioner was a Yorkshireman. Only Lancashire across the Pennines could contest the title as the home of the hangman.

The first notable Yorkshireman to carry the mantle as chief executioner was James Berry. Berry had in fact replaced another Yorkshire executioner, the bungling Barthomolew Binns, whose brief reign as the country's executioner was curtailed after a string of botched executions in 1883–4. Binns was a resident in Dewsbury when he set out on a career which saw him travel the country carrying out the full sentence of the law. He made a hash of a job at Liverpool in the spring of 1884, one of many in his short reign, and the man whom he had beaten to the post of hangman a few months earlier was then offered his job.

James Berry was a native of Heckmondwike who had served as a policeman in both Yorkshire and Nottingham before applying to be an executioner. He became famous as the official who tried to execute John Lee, 'The man they couldn't hang', in February 1885. Lee had been convicted of the murder of his employer and was taken to Exeter Gaol for execution. On the appointed morning he was led onto the scaffold where he was pinioned and noosed. Berry then pushed the lever but the trapdoors failed to open. Lee was removed whilst the gallows were retested and found to work perfectly. Three times the scene was played out and in each instance the trap failed to open with the condemned man on it. Lee was later reprieved and went on to outlive his would-be executioner. No satisfactory reason could be given for the failed hanging. Berry's reign continued through the 1880s and he too, like Binns, was credited with a fair share of bungled executions.

One of the two men who replaced Berry when he retired in 1892 was a Huddersfield rope-maker by the name of Thomas Henry Scott. Scott worked regularly as a hangman until 1902, when his name disappeared from the list of approved executioners. The man who replaced him, Henry Pierrepoint, was the first in probably the most famous dynasty of hangmen.

Pierrepoint was born at Clayton, Bradford, and carried out his first job in the winter of 1901. For close on ten years he vied with several

Lancashire men, the Billington brothers of Bolton and Rochdale barber John Ellis, to be the chief executioner of Great Britain. Pierrepoint, who had moved to Huddersfield, resigned in 1910 and was replaced by his brother Thomas who had been his assistant since 1906.

Tom Pierrepoint was to become one of the longest-serving hangmen of all time. He lived for much of his life at Town End, Bradford, before moving across town to Lidget Green. Amongst his early assistants was fellow Bradfordian Albert Lumb, who helped carry out a number of executions for a short period before 1914.

Tom Pierrepoint, sometimes assisting his brother, was the hangman at every execution at Wakefield Gaol, when for a ten-year period up to the middle of the Great War it took over from the Leeds as the hanging town for Yorkshire. It was Tom Pierrepoint who hanged most of the infamous criminals in the years prior to the Second World War, and his diary included names such as Alfred Rouse, 'the blazing car murderer'; Dr Buck Ruxton; Nurse Waddingham; and Charlotte Bryant. He also hanged many of the spies captured during the war and was the hangman appointed by the Americans to execute US servicemen convicted of crimes in the UK.

Tom retired in 1946, shortly after the death of his wife. He was 76 years old when he hung up his ropes, evidently much against his will, and was credited with over 300 executions. He had been working in a local foundry since his 60th birthday, after giving up his carter's business. He died in Bradford, on 10th February 1954, aged 84, at the home of his only daughter.

The third member of the Pierrepoint family to become a hangman was Albert Pierrepoint, born like his father in Bradford. Albert graduated from the hangmen's training school at London's Pentonville Prison in 1932 and for close on 25 years became probably the most famous executioner of modern times. He received notoriety when he executed numerous well-known criminals during and after the Second World War, although unlike his father and uncle, he had by this time made his home in Manchester. It is surprising to learn that Albert made only one visit to Armley Gaol, Leeds, to carry out an execution. This was in 1953, when he dispatched Philip Henry, a soldier who committed a brutal murder at York.

Once Albert Pierrepoint had become chief executioner he was more often than not assisted by Doncaster motor-coach dealer Stephen Wade. Wade had applied for the position of hangman in 1918, after coming out of the army, because, in his words, he hated murder. He

Stephen Wade.

was 21 at the time and was told by the prison authorities that he was too young for the position. Resolutely, he made subsequent applications over the next 20 years before finally being accepted for training shortly after the outbreak of war. 'I was never nervous,' he once wrote. 'It's a job which needs a special type of temperament. You're either fit to do it or you're not. And you soon find out!'

Wade attended a training course at Pentonville in the summer of 1940 and one of his early engagements was to help hang George

Armstrong, the first Briton hanged for treason during the war. Three months later he assisted Albert Pierrepoint on his first job as senior executioner (number one, as the post was known in the profession) and he also assisted him a few weeks later when they hanged Karel Richter, the spy who, as Pierrepoint later recalled in his biography, gave him his most difficult experience on the scaffold. Wade helped both Pierrepoints regularly during the war and was present at the executions of several spies and at Pentonville Prison in October 1945 when five Germans were hanged for the infamous 'Comrie Camp Murder'.

In March 1946 Stephen Wade was promoted to number one when he replaced Tom Pierrepoint as the hangman for Durham Prison. Wade took over as the regular number one at Leeds in the following year and was promoted to the country's chief executioner when Albert Pierrepoint retired in 1955, but a combination of illness and the temporary suspension of all executions during 1956 saw the end of his career. He retired through ill health early in 1956 and died in December of that year, at the age of 59.

The last Yorkshireman to work as an executioner was Harry Smith. Smith lived for a while as a neighbour to Stephen Wade in Doncaster and he applied to join the list of executioners in 1950. His first job was as a trainee, when he watched Albert Pierrepoint hang Nicholas Crosby at Manchester. Crosby, a young gypsy, had been convicted of the brutal murder of Ruth Massey in Leeds. Smith was present at the execution of a number of notorious killers in the 1950s, including John Christie. He also worked as a hangman in Cyprus when a number of EOKA terrorists were hanged there during the troubles.

It was in December 1875 that the gallows first crashed open at Armley Gaol, Leeds, and during the next 94 years a total of 92 men and one woman paid for their crimes on the end of the hangman's rope.

Initially, executions in Yorkshire had been carried out at York Castle but when York stopped performing executions in 1896 convicted murderers were sent to Leeds. All told, there were four centres of execution that served the area, and convicts were usually sent to the nearest gaol for execution. The rule seemed to be that those convicted in the north of Yorkshire were sent to York or to Hull; those from the south were executed at Leeds or Wakefield.

There was a rare mishap at Armley Gaol in 1877, when a hangman named Askern bungled an execution and the prisoner, a man called Johnson, had to be re-placed on the trapdoor when the rope snapped at the first attempt to hang him. A similar incident was narrowly avoided over 70 years later when a rope broke whilst Stephen Wade was testing the drop prior to Dennis Neville's execution (see Chapter 7).

Probably the most famous Victorian murderer to fall through the trap at Armley was Sheffield murderer, Charlie Peace, whose crimes have been well documented elsewhere.

In 1900 Charles Buckhouse was hanged for the murder of a policeman at Swinton. He was the first of a number of men hanged for the murders of policemen in the region. Buckhouse was hanged alongside another man who had killed his children at Holbeck. This was very nearly the last triple execution carried out in Great Britain: Buckhouse's brother was reprieved only a day or so before the execution.

There is an interesting anecdote concerning an execution that took place at Armley in 1905. The case involved a man named Tattersall, who was employed as a plasterer at Wakefield Gaol; indeed, his job was to help build the new gallows at the prison. In the summer of 1905 he was convicted and hanged for the murder of his wife. Had he carried out the crime a few months later, he would quite probably have been hanged on the very gallows he helped to build.

This execution also saw an incident that caused the death of the executioner in charge. John Billington fell through the trapdoor whilst preparing the drop. He was able to carry out his duties as planned but died from his injuries a few weeks later.

A selection of the more interesting cases which ended with the killers taking the short walk to the gallows at Armley have been included in this casebook, but one case I have not covered in detail here (like the case of Charlie Peace, it has been thoroughly documented elsewhere) is the last execution carried out by Stephen Wade.

This took place at Armley Gaol in August 1955, when Wade hanged Alec Wilkinson for the murder of his mother-in-law at Wombwell, Barnsley. The case caused massive interest in the region, with many believing that the man should not have hanged. The brief facts were that Wilkinson blamed his mother-in-law for the break-up of his marriage and in a drunken temper he stabbed her. There was evidence that the crime may have been carried out in self-defence, but even stronger was the plea of provocation. Nevertheless Wilkinson, a miner, was sentenced to death and hanged. He was able to find the strength to joke with his executioners as he was led to the drop, claiming that at least he knew where he was going and that he could use a shovel – a reference to hell and his previous job down the mines!

1

MÉNAGE
À TROIS

The Murder of William Swann at Barnsley,
June 1903

William and Emily Swann lived in George Square, at Wombwell, Barnsley. They had been married for over 20 years and had raised 11 children, when sometime in 1902 they took a lodger, a 30 year old miner named John Gallagher who worked locally at the Mitchell Main Colliery.

Within a short time Gallagher, a native of Middlesbrough and a former soldier who had been discharged from the West Yorkshire Regiment for misconduct, began an affair with his 42 year old landlady. Her husband, a 44 year old glassblower working at Aldham Glass Bottle Works, soon became suspicious of goings-on at his home while he worked the night shift, and early in 1903, he ordered Gallagher to leave the house.

Over the next few weeks, Gallagher paid regular visits back to George Square, and each visit usually ended with threats and fights between the two men. As if to make the situation worse, Gallagher then took lodgings with a Mrs Lavinia Ward, who also lived on George Square, directly opposite the Swann household.

On Saturday 6th June, Gallagher and Mrs Swann were drinking at his lodgings. Also in the house were Mrs Ward's daughter, Rose, and another lodger named Wigglesworth. Both Gallagher and Mrs Swann were quite drunk and when they had finished all the beer in the house, Gallagher sent Rose out on an errand. When Rose returned, Gallagher walked Mrs Swann home, but no sooner had he settled back down in his parlour, than Emily reappeared with a shawl over her face. She then sat down, removed the shawl and revealed a black eye.

'See what our Bill has done,' she said to those assembled, to which Gallagher replied that he would 'go and give him something for himself – I will kick his ribs in!'

He then left the house, followed by Mrs Swann and Wigglesworth and a neighbour named John Dunn, to whom Mrs Swann said: 'I hope he punches him to death, and I hope he kills the bastard.'

Gallagher reached the house and shook the door violently until it swung open. He entered, uttering that he would 'coffin Swann before the morning!' Mrs Swann also entered the house and as the other lodgers followed behind, they heard her shout 'Give it to the bastard, Johnny.'

The struggle between William Swann and John Gallagher lasted some ten minutes, after which, Gallagher returned outside and boasted that he had broken four of his ribs and would break four more. Gallagher and Mrs Swann then went back into the house, where further sounds of a struggle were heard. Ten minutes later the couple stood hand in hand at the door, before Gallagher left to go home.

Only a few minutes later Mrs Swann came back across to the Ward household and asked if Mrs Ward would come over to her house as her husband was dead. William Swann was found lying in the back kitchen, his head propped up against a cupboard. Lying beside the body was a bloodstained poker.

By the time police descended en masse on the house in George Square, Gallagher had fled. Mrs Swann was taken into custody and held on remand as a manhunt was launched. Gallagher had told witnesses during the attack that he would 'go to Bradford' after teaching Swann a lesson, but despite a search of the town, he was to remain at liberty for many weeks.

An autopsy was held the following day and it was found that the victim had sustained a frightful beating. Dr George Atkins, the pathologist, decided that death had been due to a brain haemorrhage, and although there was no fracture to the skull, there was severe bruising around the head; four ribs had been broken, as had the breastbone. It was thought that the injuries had either been caused by a severe kicking or had been inflicted with the poker found beside the body.

On the following Wednesday the funeral of William Swann took place and although his widow asked to be allowed to attend, so great was the public's outrage against her that she was forbidden to do so for her own safety. Crowds of up to eight people deep lined the road to the cemetery.

John Gallagher.

For two months after the murder, Gallagher tramped around north Yorkshire, having pawned his clothing to obtain money for food. On 4th August, half starved and 'out on his feet', he turned up in his native Middlesbrough where he was arrested at his sister's home.

Following his arrest Gallagher was charged with wilful murder and on the following day it was announced that both Gallagher and Mrs Swann would stand trial together at West Riding Assizes.

Mr Justice Darling presided over the trial on Wednesday 9th December. Mr Tindall Atkinson KC, leading for the Crown, said that the facts of the case were not in dispute: 'It is perfectly clear that the victim was done to death in his own house by violence and it was perfectly clear that no one else was in the house and could have dealt this violence except for the two prisoners at the bar.'

He also showed that there was ill feeling between the two men on account of Swann's suspicions, which were later confirmed, that Gallagher was involved in a 'ménage à trois' with Swann and his wife.

Mr Atkinson said he would point to statements made by a number of witnesses that supported the case that the two accused had been in collusion at the time when Gallagher had administered a fearful beating, and that at no time did Mrs Swann try to stop him; on the contrary, she fully supported and encouraged the attack.

Leading for the defence, Mr Mitchell Innes KC vainly tried to show that Gallagher had gone to the house merely to admonish the husband for the brutal beating of his wife. He also explained that the 'murder' had not been premeditated; rather, it had been inflamed by passion, excitement and drink. 'Gallagher', Mr Innes said, 'overdid his role as a natural avenger and protector. At no time did he intend to commit murder.'

Summing up the case, Mr Justice Darling stated that if it could be found that the killing had been committed under great provocation, then there might be reasonable grounds for a verdict of manslaughter; but where was there evidence of such provocation? He also pointed to the evidence that Mrs Swann had taken an active part in the killings, not necessarily by her immediate actions but by her verbal encouragements, as had been testified by a number of witnesses.

The jury retired for just 40 minutes before returning their verdict: they found both the accused guilty as charged. Asked if they had anything to say before sentence of death was passed, Gallagher declined, but Mrs Swann rose to her feet and declared: 'Yes! I am innocent. I am not afraid of immediate death because I am innocent and will go to God!'

Emily Swann.

Before passing sentence, the judge told the court that he had a vital piece of evidence which the prosecution had held back during the trial. It came in the form of a statement made by Gallagher after his arrest, in which he claimed that Mrs Swann had killed her husband by striking him with a poker after he (Gallagher) had punched and kicked the man to the ground. Whilst this did not prove that Mrs Swann had killed her husband, in view of the medical evidence that the poker had been used in the murder, the judge said that he was satisfied that Mrs Swann had played an active part in the murder and was therefore equally to blame for the consequences.

On Tuesday morning, 29th December, Gallagher and Emily Swann were hanged together at Armley Gaol, Leeds. According to hangman John Ellis, who assisted William Billington in carrying out the sentence, Mrs Swann had believed she would be reprieved and when word reached the prison on the day before the execution that the Home Secretary had declined mercy, she collapsed in a fit of hysteria. Gallagher, having stoically accepted his fate, never expected a reprieve.

Ellis described Mrs Swann as a short, stumpy, round-faced woman, standing a little under five feet tall and weighing slightly under nine stone. The couple had been kept apart since conviction, their only meeting being at a short service in the prison chapel on Christmas Day. They next met when they stood side by side on the gallows.

As the procession to the scaffold was formed, Mrs Swann was found to be lying prostrate on her cell floor, overcome with terror, but when they took their places on the trapdoor she had regained enough composure to speak to her lover for the last time.

'Good morning, John,' she said to her hooded companion.

'Good morning, love,' he replied as the hangman placed the rope around his neck.

'Goodbye, love, God bless you,' she whispered as Billington darted to the lever to spring the trap and William Swann was avenged.

Mrs Swann had the dubious honour of being the only woman to pay the supreme penalty on the gallows at Armley Gaol.

2

PARTNERS
IN CRIME

The Murder of Rhoda Walker at Pontefract,
August 1918

Widow Rhoda Walker had kept her late husband's silversmith's shop going in her home in Mill Hill Road, Town End, Pontefract, one of two houses standing close to the junction with the busy road to Wakefield, Barnsley and Doncaster.

At 62 years old, she was a frail woman, prone to bilious attacks; afraid of being left alone in the house, she kept a small dog for companionship, and took a lodger, a young bank clerk named Gertrude Lawn. There had been a number of staff employed at the shop but when each was in turn called up to serve in the war, Mrs Walker continued to run the sales part of the business and chose to do the repair work herself in the small workshop on the premises.

Shortly after 2 pm on Friday 16th August 1918, Gertrude Lawn left the shop to go into Pontefract. When she returned at 4.20 pm she found the shop door locked. Her suspicions were heightened when she noticed that the front shop window had been disturbed. The adjacent front door was also locked and having made her way around the back, she entered through the back door and found Mrs Walker lying on the kitchen floor.

The old woman had suffered a terrible beating: her clothes were saturated in blood that seeped from horrific head-wounds. There was a gaping wound in her forehead, her jaw was fractured in two places, she had two black eyes and the fingers of her left hand were broken. Despite the injuries, Mrs Walker was still alive and she was hurried to the local hospital where she drifted in and out of consciousness until she died in the early hours of Saturday morning.

Before she died, the old woman muttered the phrase 'Oh, George, don't' a number of times. It was to prove a vital piece of information in the investigation.

The police moved swiftly. It was clear that robbery was the motive; the ransacked window display and empty jewellery cases were testament to this. Witnesses came forward to state that two men had been seen loitering outside the shop on the afternoon of the murder. Both wore the uniforms of the Army Service Corps. Again detectives were furnished with a vital clue. One witness told detectives that she had noticed one of the men sporting six of the distinctive 'wound stripes' awarded to servicemen injured in battle.

On the following Tuesday the funeral of Mrs Walker took place, and on the same day two men were picked up in London. Investigations by officers in Pontefract had led police to the home at nearby Ackworth of Mrs Annie Pratt, the sister of 22 year old George Walter Cardwell, an army deserter, who was known to be an acquaintance of the dead woman.

Their inquiries led them to Cardwell's mother's house at Halifax and on to London, where he was arrested along with a fellow deserter Percy George Barrett, as they tried to sell items of jewellery in a public house. The belief that the goods they were selling had come from Pontefract was substantiated by the fact that many still bore price tickets easily identifiable as belonging to the murdered woman. Also, and just as damning, several of the price tickets were smeared with blood.

The large crowd that gathered at Pontefract booed and hissed at the two men as they were returned from London by train. On the following day they appeared at a hurriedly arranged sitting at the local magistrates' court, where after evidence was given they were remanded pending further inquiries.

The trial of George Cardwell and Percy Barrett took place before Mr Justice Horace Avory on Tuesday 3rd December 1918. It lasted less than a day. Both pleaded not guilty to the charges, but ignorant of the laws of guilt by association, they condemned themselves by their own mouths by each trying to pass the blame onto the other.

Leading for the Crown, Mr Charles Mellor KC outlined the evidence before the packed courtroom. On the afternoon of Friday 16th August, Mrs Walker was found badly beaten in the kitchen behind her jeweller's shop. She subsequently died from her injuries. Witnesses saw two men, alleged to be the two men in the dock, loitering around the shop on that afternoon. The crime must have taken place between the time Mrs Walker was last seen alive at around 4 pm, and 20 minutes later when Miss Lawn returned home.

On the following day detectives went to the home of Cardwell's mother where a number of items of the stolen jewellery were recovered. In a suburb of east London, close to Barrett's home, both men were picked up trying to dispose of further stolen items which were in Cardwell's possession.

Upon arrest Barrett claimed that the jewellery had been stolen in Pontefract. A few days later he made a further statement that implicated him in the murder, and again in November he made a statement to the Governor at Armley which was read in court:

> Cardwell was in the shop when the postwoman went in. When he went in he hid in the parlour because there was nobody in the shop at the time, and also because he saw the shadow of someone looking through the window. He told me that when the postwoman went in, he heard someone coming in through the back way and he made a rush towards the kitchen door, thinking it was a man but it was Mrs Walker. After leaving Ackworth we got a train to Wakefield and arrived at his mother's house about 12 o'clock. He washed his clothes next day which were covered in blood . . .

Evidence was then heard from several women who had been near the shop that afternoon, including the postwoman, who had entered the shop, shouted 'post' and after leaving a letter on the counter had walked out without seeing the owner.

A further statement made by Barrett was read out in which he claimed that when he entered the shop Mrs Walker was on the floor, gagged with Cardwell's handkerchief. At Cardwell's request he had fetched a cushion to put over her mouth which seemed to stop her breathing. This statement had ended with Barrett declaring: 'I can honestly say that I did not touch Mrs Walker.'

Barrett reiterated much of what he had claimed in his statements when he took his place in the dock, but when Cardwell followed him, the courtroom heard a very different account of what had happened that afternoon.

Cardwell, a native of Brighouse, told the court that he had been released from Borstal in 1915 after serving a sentence for stealing from gas meters. At the age of 17, in May 1915, he had joined the colours and

The two army deserters, George Cardwell and Percy Barrett, were hanged side by side at Armley Gaol, Leeds on 8th January 1919.

went to France where he was wounded once and gassed five times. He was subsequently passed unfit for service and transferred to the Army Service Corps, but not before he had been recommended for a Distinguished Conduct Medal and Military Medal for bravery. He had deserted from his unit because he felt that if he was fit to be in the ASC then he was fit to return to France.

He had become friendly with Barrett, and the two of them had gone to stay with Cardwell's sister at Ackworth and found work at Hemsworth colliery, stating that they were awaiting the call-up.

He said that on the day of the murder he had dressed in his uniform and gone to the Pontefract jeweller's to buy a watch key, without any intention of committing a crime. He said that Barrett had entered the shop first, but as he knew the old woman, who may have been aware that he was posted as a deserter, Cardwell chose to wait outside. He said he saw his friend's bloodstained hand reach into the window and snatch some items. Barrett was then alleged to have come out of the shop and said: 'We will have to get away from here, I have killed the old woman.'

This version of events seemed to be more likely, given that a witness had said that she had seen a soldier with wound stripes standing alone outside during the afternoon. However, Mrs Walker's last words would

Tom Pierrepoint. He hanged 31 people at Leeds.

seem to implicate Cardwell as being at least in the shop at some stage. Regardless of which version was true, as the law stood, both were deemed equally as guilty since, as it was put across in court, 'both had been prepared to benefit from a share of the spoils'.

The jury retired for just seven minutes before returning a guilty verdict. Donning the black cap, Mr Justice Avory stated that he had never had a more painful duty than to pass sentence on two such young men, but this was the sentence that must inevitably follow the crime for which they had been committed.

On Wednesday 8th January the two young deserters were hanged side by side at Armley Gaol by Tom Pierrepoint. Cardwell had penned a last letter to his father stating that he was innocent and had been convicted on a coward's statement.

3

A
TRIFLING MILITARY MATTER

The Murder of Private Leslie White near Leyburn,
May 1929

Tuesday 14th May 1929 was a pleasant late spring morning as the military escort passed through the quiet village of Constable Burton, returning their prisoner to Catterick Army Camp. Driving the Crossley military tender was Sergeant William Brett of the 4th Battalion Tank Corps; beside him in the cab was Sergeant Prangnell, whilst on the back of the truck sat Private Leslie White with their prisoner Private Arthur Leslie Raveney.

Raveney, a 24 year old Londoner with a wife living in Hartlepool, had been picked up by police in Bedale after being listed as absent without leave, and he was being returned to camp to face what would surely be a stiff sentence for the second breach of military discipline in the last fortnight.

As the tender passed through Constable Burton, Sergeant Prangnell heard a sound that he took to be a blown tyre and told the driver to slow down. As they did so, Sergeant Brett looked through his rear window and saw the prisoner leap over the tailgate and set off at great speed in the direction they had just travelled. They watched him for a distance of 200 yards before he disappeared over the horizon.

Looking into the van, the driver was horrified to see Private White lying seriously wounded. 'He has shot me,' the wounded soldier managed to whisper. Brett and Prangnell headed for the local village in search of medical help, where they were informed that the nearest doctor could be found at Leyburn; here White was attended by Doctor Peacock. His diagnosis did not offer much encouragement, and he suggested they would do better to return to the Catterick camp hospital.

Private Leslie White and Private Arthur Raveney.

The escort returned in haste to Catterick where Private White was admitted with a severe abdomen wound. He died shortly after arrival.

Police in nearby Richmond were alerted by camp authorities, and messages were sent to police in both Northallerton and Leyburn. All available officers in the area were sent out in search of the deserter, and officers from the flying squad at York were also dispatched to the area.

Under the control of the Chief Constable, Major Bower, Sergeant Prangnell led a group of officers to the scene of the murder, where they combed the area in case Raveney had gone to ground close by. However, word soon reached back that he had been sighted in nearby Finghall.

The manhunt lasted seven hours, during which time Raveney discarded his tunic and cap. He was reported by witnesses as vaulting fences with the skill of an 'Olympic hurdler' as he made good his escape, but eventually he succumbed to exhaustion. As darkness closed in, a posse of over 30 armed officers supplemented by many civilians cornered the fugitive at Rockwith Quarry near Newton-le-Willows. He was then taken to Leyburn police station and charged with murder.

On the following day a haggard-looking prisoner appeared before Leyburn magistrates' court where he was remanded to Armley Gaol, Leeds. An inquest on the murdered soldier was held 24 hours later which concluded that a gunshot wound had punctured both the liver and kidney and that the bullet had embedded itself in the spinal muscles. Concluding the inquest, the pathologist stated: 'I am of the opinion that the cause of death was haemorrhage following loss of blood due to a bullet wound.'

The seven-hour trial at York Assizes before Mr Justice Mackinnon, on Monday 9th July 1929, was little more than a formality; the main point of dispute seemed to concern a motive. It was claimed that there was bad feeling between the prisoner and the victim which seemed to have stemmed from an incident earlier that year.

Prosecuting counsel, Mr C. F. Lowenthal KC, stated that sometime before the alleged murder Raveney had been acting as an officer's servant, but had been transferred back to ordinary duties after a 'trifling military matter'.

On 11th May, he was back on ordinary duty and was issued with a service revolver which, it was suggested, was the murder weapon. Raveney was then confined to barracks for going absent without leave and put under the charge of Private White. It was during this time that some ill feeling may have arisen between the two men.

Describing events on the day of the shooting, prosecuting counsel said that the crime took place as Raveney was being transferred back to camp having been picked up as an absentee from his unit by police in Bedale. He was searched by police officers at Bedale before the escorting party arrived, but no weapon was found on him. The police officer who conducted the search was forced to admit in court that he had made only a frisk of his pockets, and if the weapon had been concealed under his armpit, as was suggested, then he would not have noticed it.

Giving evidence in his defence, Raveney said that he had been issued the revolver on 11th May, but on the following day he found it had been stolen. He decided not to report it yet, but to take some 'French leave' before returning to face up to the AWOL charge and to report the loss of his weapon.

Raveney said they had travelled some distance in the rear of the lorry when he became cramped and tried to change his position. White was alleged to have made some remark to the prisoner, to which he replied that if he had wanted to escape he could have done so by now.

'I was putting my hand in my overcoat pocket to get a cigarette when I looked around at White and saw that he drawn his revolver and that it was loaded,' Raveney stated.

White was then alleged to have said: 'If you try that you will have some of this coming', indicating his revolver.

'I was astonished and realised that I was in a dangerous position,' Raveney continued. 'White's hand was shaking so much and with the least pressure, with the gun cocked, I felt it would go off. With my left hand I brushed the revolver lightly aside and grabbed White's right hand. At the same moment I grabbed the barrel and turned it away, but at that moment the van went around a corner and we swayed together. It was here that the gun went off.'

Addressing the jury for the defence, Mr A. R. Lindsay told them that there were three possible verdicts in this case: guilty of murder, guilty of manslaughter, and not guilty.

'Whatever you believe this man be guilty of', he pleaded, 'it is not murder. It might be manslaughter, but if you believe his story then I ask you to acquit him.'

Clearly believing the prosecution's version of events that Raveney had shot White with the gun he had concealed about him, rather than that he was shot by his own gun during a struggle, the jury needed just a short absence to find Raveney guilty as charged.

Asked if he had anything to say before sentence was passed, the prisoner said: 'I think myself that there are certain points that want to be gone into further in the evidence against me.' Raveney's wife then sobbed hysterically as the judge passed sentence of death on her husband.

An appeal against the conviction was heard and rejected; a similar fate greeted a petition for a reprieve to the Home Secretary. Raveney maintained a cheerful demeanour in the death cell, claiming that the death of Private White was an accident.

On Wednesday 14th August, Private Arthur Leslie Raveney became the 59th person to be executed at Armley Gaol.

4

TOO MANY TELL-TALE CLUES

The Murder of Mark Turner at Halifax, *April 1943*

For over 40 years Mark Turner had worked as a postman in and around Halifax, before finally, in March 1922, he received his long-service medal and settled happily into retirement. He was an exceptionally well-read and kindly man, and it was his kind nature and willingness to help others less fortunate than himself that was to cost him his life.

It was on the afternoon of Saturday 3rd April 1943 that his battered body was found when, concerned for his whereabouts, neighbours asked the police to visit his home at 1 Moorfield Street, Halifax. A widower for many years, 82 year old Turner had also survived his two daughters, and he had for a long time lived alone in the small terraced house.

Entering the house, Police Constable Crisp found the old man's body in a folding settee bed: he had been battered around the head with a hammer. Searching the house, police found a vital piece of evidence linking a man with the murder.

Hidden in Turner's home were various parts of a soldier's attire, including a tunic with an army number inside. The number, A29600, was found to belong to a 35 year old private in the Canadian Ordnance Corps, Mervin Clare McEwen. A description of McEwen was issued in which he was described as being tall and well built, with brushed back brown hair and a ruddy complexion. He spoke with a Scottish accent and it was believed he was half Scot-half Canadian; he had absconded from his unit in the south of England in February.

Missing from the house were a quantity of cash; ration books and

1 Moorfield Street, once the home of Mark Turner.

identity cards in the name of the murdered man; his gold watch and a briefcase marked 'M.T. HX'.

From interviewing Turner's friends and neighbours police learned that the deserter had been living rough in Savile Park, Halifax for a few days before the murder and that the old man had shown kindness to him by offering him, on more than one occasion, a room and refreshments at his house.

Eighty-four year old William Crabtree, a friend of the victim, told Chief Inspector Griffiths, who had taken charge of the investigation, that he and Turner had befriended the soldier and that on the night prior to the murder he had left the two of them at Turner's house. A neighbour said that in the early hours of that morning, he heard a knocking sound from inside the house, but thinking it might be someone shutting a door, he thought no more about it.

The investigation into the whereabouts of the wanted soldier went on for nearly two months and shifted from Yorkshire across to Manchester, where sightings of the man were reported. McEwen was eventually found in the company of a woman he had met at Manchester railway station on the morning following the murder. He was living under the alias of James Acton, a discharged seaman.

Mark Turner.

Taken into custody, McEwen was found to be in possession of ration and identity cards belonging to Mark Turner. Having been taken back to Halifax, the prisoner said that he wanted to make a statement with regard to the crime.

McEwen said that after leaving the two old men he had returned to the park, but had become hungry and returned to Moorfield Street, with the intention of stealing some food. As he was taking the food, the old man woke up and he had picked up the hammer to stop him from crying out. He then picked up a knife and had stabbed him through the bedclothes to 'shut him up'.

Savile Park, where McEwen had been sleeping rough.

Furnished with a full confession, Mr G. H. B. Streatfeild KC, the prosecution counsel, made short work of McEwen's defence when he stood before Mr Justice Stable at Leeds Assizes in December. When faced with the statement that he had battered the old man, McEwen admitted that he had hit him once, but said that he had no recollection of carrying out any further attacks, claiming his memory was vague after drinking a lot of neat whisky. Streatfeild claimed that McEwen's guilt had been established by the evidence left at the scene – 'too many tell-tale clues' he called it – that linked the prisoner to the murder.

McEwen's counsel, Mr Paley Scott KC, suggested that it was hunger and drink that caused the accused to return to the house and force an entry. He asked the jury to consider that McEwen was so incapacitated with drink that he was incapable of forming the necessary intention to commit murder. He ended his case by stating that the correct verdict in this case should be one of manslaughter.

Summing up the evidence, Mr Justice Stable touched upon the subject of drink by saying that if the jury believed the accused's own version of events, then they must return a verdict of wilful murder. It was no answer to a charge, he stated, to say that a man had taken drink and that because he was drunk he did something he would not do

Mervin Clare McEwen.

when sober. But, where the charge was murder and there was evidence which led to the conclusion that the man was deprived of his faculties so as to be incapable of forming the intention to kill or to do serious bodily harm, or evidence that he was in a drunken delirium or frenzy and struck the blow without intent to do serious injury, then the verdict could be manslaughter.

The jury took 40 minutes to find the Canadian guilty of wilful murder, and on 3rd February 1944, Mervin McEwen, the killer who left too many tell-tale clues, was hanged by Tom Pierrepoint and assistant Stephen Wade at Armley Gaol.

5

INTO
THE BIG LEAGUE

The Murders of Percy and Alice Baker at Standedge,
May 1947

The somewhat grandly named Manor House Farm at Standedge Pass stood on the main A62 road linking Oldham in Lancashire and Huddersfield, Yorkshire. Almost on the border of the two counties, it offered picturesque views of the desolate Saddleworth Moors. It was here that Percy and Alice Baker, both in their early forties, disappeared suddenly in the late spring of 1947.

The couple had a weekly routine of sharing Sunday lunch with their friends Mr and Mrs Leonard Doughty. If the Doughtys hadn't called at Manor House Farm by 2 pm, then the Bakers would walk the two miles down the road and lunch with their friends across the border at their home in Dobcross.

This routine had been broken on Sunday 25th May 1947, when the Bakers failed to come for lunch. On the following day Mrs Baker also failed to show up for a meeting with her friend Mrs Buckley, and a few days later Mrs Buckley decided to call on her friends to check everything was well.

She walked the short distance to the farmhouse and was more than a little surprised to see a furniture van outside the front gates. The crest on the van bore the name 'Gold Lea & Co.', with an address in Oldham. As Mrs Buckley approached the front door two men came out of the house carrying a sofa.

Asked by Mrs Buckley if her friend was replacing her suite, the older of the two men put down the heavy settee and after wiping his brow replied: 'No, they're moving.'

Clearly taken aback, Mrs Buckley told the man that her friend hadn't

Manor House Farm.

mentioned anything about moving, to which he just shrugged his shoulders and continued about his work.

'That's strange. They've only been here since September, and only a short time ago they were both telling us how much they liked living here,' Mrs Buckley said, as she stood in the gateway blocking the men's path to the van.

'Look, they've split up,' the older man said as Mrs Buckley looked on bewildered. 'That's what he told me. He came into my shop last Thursday and said he and his wife had separated and that he wanted to sell the furniture. He was going back to the RAF. . . I've got the signed agreement from Mr Baker at my office.'

As the removal men went about their task, Mrs Buckley returned home and contacted her husband at work. He agreed that it sounded suspicious and said he would speak to the Doughtys, who he knew had arranged to have lunch with the Bakers the previous Sunday.

'Leonard Doughty knows the Bakers better than us, he'll know what's going on,' he told his wife.

When Buckley phoned Doughty that evening his friend confirmed that the Bakers had failed to show up on Sunday and they had not heard anything since. On the following day Ernest Buckley and Leonard Doughty went to the offices of 'Gold Lea & Co.' in Oldham and spoke to the proprietor, Philip Libman, one of the men Mrs Buckley had seen emptying the house on the previous day.

He showed the two men the receipt signed by Mr Baker and at once Doughty spoke up. 'I've known Percy Baker for twenty years, and I can assure you that is not his signature.'

Asked to describe the man who had signed the agreement, Mr Libman said that he was a young man in his twenties with a limp. 'He showed me a scar on his left leg and told me he had been discharged from the RAF because of the injury.'

'That is not Percy Baker!' Doughty exclaimed. 'Percy's nearer to our age. He's in his early forties.'

Libman said that it was indeed suspicious as it meant that someone was going around impersonating Baker. 'And selling his furniture,' Buckley cut in. 'I think we had better call the police.'

Detective Constable Turner was dispatched to the shop and took statements from the three men, starting with Mr Libman. Libman told the officer that the man claiming to be Mr Baker had called into the shop on Thursday 22nd May. Libman said he had accompanied the man to Manor House Farm and he had opened the front door with a key. 'He asked me for £400, for the contents, but when he came into the shop on the following day we settled on £300,' Libman said, adding that they then returned to the house to make a full inventory.

Asked if had noticed anything unusual, Libman said that there were some rings and a wristwatch in the upstairs bedroom, but 'Baker' said they belonged to his wife and she must have left them behind. 'They had after all, just separated, so it did sound plausible,' he told the officer.

Libman said there was one other strange thing, and that was that a dog was locked in the shed throughout his visit, and when he asked why he didn't let it out, the man had told him it would run off and he hadn't time to chase after it.

Libman had asked for some form of identification and had been shown an identity card with the name Percy Baker. 'I gave him a deposit of £100 and yesterday my assistant and I went to collect the furniture.'

Asked if they had brought all the furniture back, Libman said that most of the stuff had been brought back but, at the man's request, some personal items had been dropped off at a shop in nearby Uppermill.

'We took about ten suitcases and a linen box there. Soon after we got to Uppermill he rode up on a bicycle and unlocked the shop so we could unload the suitcases. I then gave him the balance of the money. I told him someone had been asking about Mrs Baker . . . I asked him if he knew her address but he was evasive . . . "I'm not telling you because this man you've been talking to is the cause of our separation."'

After statements had been taken from all three, the police drove over to Manor House Farm but the place was locked up and they were unable to gain entry. They then headed for Uppermill and as they travelled down the main Standedge to Uppermill road they spotted Baker's car parked on the roadside. They tried to open it but like the house it was securely locked. They waited for a while but there was no one around.

DC Turner reported back to the station and an investigation was set up into the whereabouts of the Bakers. In the meantime PC Crooks from Uppermill took Mr Libman to find the shop where he had dropped off the suitcases. When they arrived at the shop, the constable said that he thought it was rented by a certain John Gartside.

As the two men drove out of Uppermill they spotted Baker's car again on a garage forecourt. A man was standing in front of the car, and Libman identified him as the man claiming to be Baker.

Libman and the constable approached and the man looked up in a start as he was spoken to.

'Excuse me sir, are you the owner of this vehicle?'

'Of course I am,' he replied.

'Will you tell me your name, sir?'

Up to this moment the man hadn't spotted Mr Libman behind the officer and he went pale as recognition flitted across his face. He managed to regain his composure and told the man his name was Percy Baker.

PC Crooks was one of those rural police officers who made it his business to know everybody on his beat and he knew the real identity of the man claiming to be Percy Baker.

'I know you,' he said slowly; 'your name is John Gartside.'

Despite his protestations to the contrary, Gartside was taken into custody pending further inquiries. He continued to try to bluff his way out of the situation by stating that he had impersonated Mr Baker at the man's request 'to speed up the deal with Mr Libman'; that he had

Alice and Percy Baker.

bought the car off Baker on the previous Friday for £200; and that he had bought the furniture for a similar amount a day or so later. He could show no receipts for these transactions, nor had he any evidence to back up his claims.

Detective Chief Inspector Ernie Stubbs of the West Riding CID at Wakefield was called in to oversee the case and after leaving instructions that Gartside should be held at Uppermill, he summoned the assistance of Lewis Nickolls, director of the North East Forensic Science Laboratory at Wakefield, to join him at Manor House Farm.

Nickolls pointed to a number of stains on the walls and ceiling and suggested that someone appeared to have tried to wash them. 'Looks like blood to me,' he told the inspector.

A further search of the house found more evidence suggesting that someone had been killed there and that the killer had tried to cover his tracks by cleaning up afterwards.

As the two men painstakingly examined every inch of the farm, officers were sent to Gartside's house. They found that he lived with his parents less than 300 yards away from Manor House Farm on the main Oldham to Huddersfield road. Looking out of Gartside's bedroom window, the officers could clearly see the Bakers' residence.

Leading the search at Gartside's house, Detective Sergeant Baugh

John Gartside.

found a suit that showed faint traces of what appeared to be blood, but more damning was a 0.38 Webley revolver taken from his bedside cabinet.

Gartside was interviewed by Chief Inspector Stubbs that evening and persisted with his story that he had purchased items off Mr Baker. The interview was halted when a call came through that bloodstains found at the house were proved to be human. Returning to interview Gartside, Stubbs told him that he now had proof that a murder had been committed at Manor House Farm.

Asked who had been murdered, the detective said that it must be either Mr or Mrs Baker.

'What if it is both?' Gartside said coldly.

Cautioned, he then made a rambling statement in which he claimed that he made a call to see Baker about buying the car and was offered the chance to buy some bedroom furniture. He claimed that Mrs Baker seemed to object to this but he sensed that they had been arguing before his arrival and he guessed from a remark Baker made that his wife had been having an affair.

He then said that Baker had brought a loaded rifle and revolver downstairs to show him, and put them on the hall settee. Gartside said that Mrs Baker had then come into the room in a rage and had picked up a poker, intent on striking her husband with it.

He claimed that Baker picked up the gun and shot his wife dead, whereupon Gartside tried to wrestle the gun from him and it went off, hitting Baker in the head. 'I then panicked. He was making a great deal of noise, writhing about in agony, so I picked up the rifle and shot him twice to put him out of his misery. There was blood all over the place!'

Gartside continued with his fantastic story by stating that he had then buried the bodies on the moors and made it look like they had gone away. He realised the predicament he was in and felt sure no one would believe him if he told the truth.

On the following day, police officers searched the area where Gartside claimed to have buried Mr and Mrs Baker. At a place known as Brun Moor, 200 yards from Standedge cutting, and half a mile from their home, the naked bodies of Percy and Alice Baker were found in a shallow grave.

County pathologist Dr T. L. Sutherland carried out the post-mortem and found that Percy Baker had been shot three times: twice in the head and once in the body. The calibre of bullets matched the 0.38 found in Gartside's bedroom. Mrs Baker had been shot once with a revolver and judging from the burn marks on the flesh, the shot had been fired from a few inches away.

On Monday 28th July 1947, John Gartside found himself before Mr Justice Pritchard at Leeds Assizes. His defence was handled by Mr G. R. Hinchcliffe KC, while Mr G. H. B. Streatfeild KC led for the Crown.

Although Gartside's story was incredible, he had such a plausible manner and was so self-assured that it was felt by some that he had a fair chance of convincing the jury he was innocent.

However, Mr Streatfeild had a strong case. He was able to pick away at inconsistencies in Gartside's statement. He managed to show, through police reconstruction and witness statements, that there was no sofa in the hall where Gartside claimed Baker had put the guns. He also discredited Gartside's claim that Baker had been accidentally shot during a struggle. Forensic evidence found that it was a physical impossibility for Baker to have shot himself in the head as Gartside claimed, as from the trajectory of the bullet it could not have been fired by someone who was right-handed, as Baker was.

As both counsel set out their cases, what had actually happened on that night seemed clearer. Gartside, a petty criminal, dubbed a 'spiv and a wide-boy' by his counsel, had kept an eye on the Bakers' house, seemingly waiting for the opportunity to burgle the place.

On the night in question he had gone to the house carrying his guns and during the course of a robbery he was disturbed. It was Mrs Baker who came into the house first. Confronted by the intruder, Mrs Baker began to shout for help. Gartside pulled out his gun and demanded that she 'shut up'. Instead of heeding his command she became hysterical and when he failed in his attempts to quieten her he panicked and shot her dead. Having now moved into the 'big league' as a killer, he then had no choice but to execute Percy Baker when he rushed into the house.

The Crown showed Gartside to be the callous killer he was by stating that rather than panic he coolly plotted the scheme of pretending the couple had separated and hatched a plan to pass himself off as Percy Baker.

The guilty verdict, when it came after the three-day trial, was the only possible verdict on the evidence presented and Gartside was sentenced to death in the prescribed manner.

There was no appeal and one month later, on Thursday 21st August, the 'spiv and wide-boy' who had made an unsuccessful promotion into the 'big league' was hanged by Stephen Wade at Armley Gaol.

6

THE
MADNESS OF 'LUCKY GEORGE'?

The Murders of Alison, Joyce and Maurice Parkin
at Doncaster,
October 1947

'Come quickly, something horrible has happened,' the woman shouted across the street to her neighbour. It was shortly after midday on Friday 10th October 1947, when Mrs Corcoran noticed that the back door of the house belonging to her neighbour, a Mrs Parkin on Wainwright Road, Doncaster, was standing open. It had been like this for a few hours and worried about the family's welfare, she had gone to investigate. She was familiar with her neighbour's day-to-day routine and knew that normally, at lunchtime, the whole family should have been at work.

What she found when she stepped inside would haunt her for the rest of her life. On the kitchen floor she stumbled across the body of 15 year old Maurice Parkin. The kitchen showed signs of a fight and the young lad's features were grotesquely distorted; his tongue hung from his bloated and battered face, showing clear signs of strangulation.

Horrified, she hurried outside and summoned the assistance of her neighbour, Mr Widdiwiss, who joined her at the house. Seeing the young lad on the floor, he wasted no time in calling the police, and as officers searched the rest of the house they encountered a truly terrible scene.

In the adjoining living room were the bodies of Maurice's mother and sister, 49 year old Alison Parkin, a widow, and 23 year old Joyce Parkin. They too had been strangled, but this was only revealed at the later post-mortem. Cause of death in the case of the two women was initially

39

Alison Parkin's house in Wainwright Road, Doncaster.

hard to estimate as both had been stripped and subjected to brutal sexual mutilation with a knife. Faeces, urine and blood were smeared across the bodies, on the furniture nearby and on the bedding upstairs. Two bloodstained knives were also recovered from the bedroom.

Once detectives had converged on the house and spoken to neighbours, they quickly had a prime suspect: Mrs Parkin's sometime boyfriend George Whelpton, who worked at the local bus garage.

Blessed with a fine physique and good looks, George Whelpton had never had a problem with women. The 31 year old bus driver seemed to be able to have his pick of available women in his home town of Doncaster. He was a popular man with many friends in the town he had proudly returned to after serving with distinction with the 'Desert Rats'. It had been in the desert that Whelpton had earned the nickname 'Lucky George' on account of the charmed life he had led in the face of enemy action.

Police were soon onto Whelpton and when they called at his mother's house in Thomson Avenue, Edlington, they learned of a strange incident that had happened earlier that morning. His mother told detectives that George had arrived home at a little after 6.30 am. He had then woken his mother and told her he was going away.

Alison Parkin.

Joyce Parkin.

'This time it really is goodbye,' he had told her, but despite words to the contrary, Whelpton had returned home at the usual time that evening and after eating his tea he had sat in silence, staring intently into the kitchen fire. Mrs Whelpton was used to George's strange behaviour, and wasn't unduly worried when he began to talk to the fire, claiming that there were 'red devils' out to get him. She told police that he had tried to swat the 'devils' with a towel before leaving the house. Such behaviour, she stressed to officers, was not unusual for George. She told police that she didn't know where he was heading other than that he had mentioned going to the bus depot to see about some money.

George Whelpton was arrested at his place of work later that night. He had called to collect his wages, and warned that the police were looking for him, staff at Armthorpe bus garage kept him talking while someone phoned the police. He was talking with colleagues when a patrol car pulled into the garage forecourt, whereupon he was quickly taken into custody.

'We are investigating the murders of Alison Parkin and two of her

41

'Lucky' George Whelpton.

children at their home, and we believe you may be able to help us with our inquiries,' Whelpton was told. He appeared to think deeply for a few moments before he replied: 'Yes, that's right I do know about it. We had a row and I did it. I just can't remember all that happened.'

Taken to the local police station and asked to elaborate on his statement, Whelpton claimed he had had a quarrel with Mrs Parkin and had hit her. Her son, awoken by the commotion, had come down, whereupon Whelpton had hit him also, and he had done the same to Joyce when she came downstairs.

'I don't remember anything more. I left the house while it was dark and caught a trackless bus to Balby and got off and went to my mother's house at Edlington.'

George Whelpton stood trial before Mr Justice Morris at Leeds in December. He was indicted only for the murder of Mrs Parkin, but evidence relating to the other murders was called on by both prosecuting and defence counsel.

Opening for the Crown, Mr Harry Hylton-Foster KC described the prisoner as 'a perfectly normal man in every respect' who had committed a murder as macabre and horrible as it was possible to recall.

Among the first witnesses called was Whelpton's mother, who told the court a little about the background of the 'beast in the dock', as he had been labelled by some.

Cross-examined by Mr Ralph Cleworth KC, for the defence, she recalled how her son had received serious head injuries in 1936 following an accident on his motor-cycle. From then on he behaved 'queerly', often after a drink, and his conduct at times terrified his family. She added that during the war he had served bravely with the Yorks and Lancashire Regiment, seeing action in Egypt and North Africa.

Whelpton's mother made a brave attempt to cover up her distress at the events which had taken place but later broke down when pathologist Dr T. L. Sutherland told the court his findings at the post-mortem.

Also speaking up for Whelpton was his wife, Irene. They had met in the summer of 1939, and when war clouds loomed heavily over the country, they had decided to marry. They soon had a child, and with Whelpton being allowed frequent home leave, the family grew until there were six children. Although the long periods of separation put a strain on their relationship, it wasn't until the husband returned to civvy street that the real cracks began to appear.

Whelpton, with his dashing good looks, developed a wandering eye. His wife had had to make what amounted to a new life for herself and the children while he was on military service, and now it seemed

Mr Harry Hylton-Foster KC.

neither of them could be bothered to make the effort to hold the marriage together. Whelpton began to spend more and more time on night shifts and went to his mother's on other nights. He had by this time begun an affair with Alison Parkin.

Despite her husband's infidelity, his wife also supported his mother's admissions that her husband was suffering from some form of insanity, and said that on a number of occasions he had passed out after drinking.

In an attempt to support a claim of insanity, events leading up to the gruesome murders were recounted by Whelpton's counsel. On the night of 9th October 1947, Whelpton had gone for a drink with Alison, along with her sister and husband. Although she was nearly 20 years older than him, Alison and George enjoyed a good relationship and he got on well with her children and friends.

There was nothing to suggest what would happen later that night when the foursome drank together in one of the local pubs. The only incident of note was when Whelpton asked the landlord to lend him a pound and offered him a wallet as security. At closing time George and Alison were given a lift to her house by her brother-in-law and they were last seen walking arm in arm together down Wainwright Road towards her front door.

Ten minutes later, at around 11.25 pm, Joyce Parkin arrived home and stood kissing her boyfriend at the front door. After a few moments her mother called from inside and they parted.

At a few minutes past six on the following morning, Stella Mitchell, a workmate of Joyce's, made her customary call to the house. Unusually, the inside of the house was in darkness, and although she tried to rouse her friend she could get no reply. She tried both doors and found them to be locked. The next person to call at the house had been Mrs Corcoran later that morning.

Following his arrest, Whelpton had made a number of statements as to what had happened in the house. In various accounts he said that after the children had gone to bed he had supper with Alison, whereupon they had gone into the sitting-room where she asked him for some money. She made a remark that her previous fellow had given her money and this started off a quarrel.

'She picked something up and tried to strike me with it. I caught hold of her and she dropped to the floor. I could not make her talk to me. I was frightened and ran outside and I met her son in the kitchen . . . I hit him . . . he fell on the floor and would not talk to me either. I then saw the daughter in the living room . . . I then hit her and I don't remember anything else.' In further statements he said that he had been upstairs in bed with Joyce when Alison had caught them.

As the trial drew to a conclusion it appeared that the main issue at stake was whether Whelpton was insane as his counsel claimed, or whether he was, as the Crown alleged, a brutal killer who had committed the terrible crimes for sexual gratification.

Summing up the case, Mr Justice Morris took a strong line against the defence of insanity, pointing out that just because there may be an absence of motive, as the defence had at one point claimed, 'that itself does not prove insanity'. Despite his wife acting on his behalf by going into the witness box, it was felt by many that this merely showed Whelpton to be a double-crossing adulterer.

The jury returned with a verdict in 20 minutes. They found Whelpton guilty as charged. Sentencing him to death, the judge added that the jury had convicted him on the clearest evidence of a terrible crime. 'Thank you,' Whelpton smiled as his fate was sealed. There was no appeal, his counsel instead hoping that the plea of insanity might be further looked into and leniency shown.

On 7th January 1948, Whelpton's luck finally ran out when he was hanged at Armley Gaol. His executioner was Doncaster coach dealer Stephen Wade, a man well known to Whelpton. Wade noted that his erstwhile friend met his end bravely.

7

A
MAN OF MISFORTUNE

The Murder of Marian Poskett at Dewsbury,
February 1949

Miner Joe Poskett was sharing a lunchtime drink with some workmates at Dewsbury Moor Working Men's Club when someone began talking excitedly at the bar about a murder that had taken place. 'They've found the body of a young girl on the field behind Calderbank Mill,' he overheard the man begin; 'the place is swarming with police.'

Poskett had an uneasy feeling, and decided to go home and see if his daughter Marian had returned after failing to come home last night. Not that he was unduly worried – 21 year old Marian often stayed over with friends after a night dancing.

When Joe Poskett arrived back at his house in Low Road, Dewsbury Moor, he was nonetheless perturbed to find that Marian had not returned, and when he ventured down to the local police station, his worst fears were confirmed.

It was a chilly Sunday morning, 20th February 1949, when dairyman Harry Hackett took his dog for a run on St Matthew's cricket field, beside the main Huddersfield to Leeds railway line behind Calderbank Mill. Approaching the field, he was ready to release his collie dog from its lead when what appeared to be a bundle of rags caught his eye. Closer inspection revealed the body of a young woman.

Hackett wasted no time summoning the police, and Superintendent Arthur Iveson of the Dewsbury Borough Police Force immediately called in assistance from the West Riding Murder Squad. Amongst the first to arrive at the scene were Detective Sergeant Harold Wynne and Dr E. G. Mahoney who examined the body on the spot.

The field by Calderbank Mill where the body of Marian Poskett was discovered.

They noted that the body was lying near a dry-stone wall which was splashed with blood. Blood had run from the girl's nose and mouth and had dried on her face. Fingernail marks and small abrasions could be clearly seen on her neck and these extended down to her right breast. The doctor also noted that the woman was partially dressed: her blouse was undone and her skirt and panties had been removed and lay beside the body. Concluding his scene-of-crime report, Dr Mahoney recorded the cause of death as strangulation and that the girl had been dead for approximately 12 hours.

Once the body had been identified as that of Marian Poskett, inquiries into her last movements were set into motion. It was soon clear that police needed to speak to a young man named Dennis Neville, who had at one time been Marian's boyfriend and who, as witnesses told police, had been seen walking towards the cricket field on the previous night.

Detective Sergeant Wynne found that Marian, after spending the earlier part of the evening at the Clarence Hotel, had gone dancing at the Galleon Ballroom, where she had a rendezvous with Dennis Neville. They were both seen in the dance-hall but not together, although a friend of Marian's saw them leave together and told police that it appeared that Dennis intended walking her home.

Police calling at the Neville household on Manor Road, West Town, discovered that Dennis had told his mother he was going to see his brother at Batley. Dewsbury police alerted their colleagues at Batley and later that Sunday evening Neville was interviewed by the police. He denied any knowledge of Marian Poskett's death, although when police asked to look at his clothes, bloodstains were clearly evident.

An autopsy on the murdered woman found that she had been three months pregnant. It was also found that she had had intercourse shortly before her death and that her jaw had been shattered with a punch.

After making further inquiries, Detective Sergeant Wynne returned to speak to Neville and said that he believed he knew more about the death of Marian Poskett than he had told them.

'Okay,' Neville said, 'forget what I said before. I did it. I will tell you the truth now.'

Neville then made a statement regarding his movements on the previous night. He said that he spent the evening in a number of public houses before meeting Marian at the Galleon Ballroom where she asked him to walk her home: 'We walked through Dewsbury, along Watergate, climbed under the railings of St Matthew's cricket field and went as far as the railway embankment. We talked for a while and then I took hold of her neck in my right hand and sunk my fingers into her throat. She laid back without making any sound. She was still breathing. I thumped her on the jaw and also in the throat with the side of my hand.' Neville was arrested and charged with the murder of Marian Poskett.

The case came to trial at Leeds on Monday 9th May 1949, and despite the confession Dennis Neville had made on arrest, his defence counsel put forward a plea of insanity and focused on his tragic background to try to justify his actions and to appeal to the sympathy of the jury.

His counsel, Mr Ralph Cleworth KC, told the court that in 1941 at the age of 14, Neville had left St Paulinus' Catholic School, and taken a job with a firm of waste-paper merchants. Being a tall, stocky youth, he was able to pass for someone much older and at the age of 15 he signed up for the army. He had served 106 days when his true age became known and he was discharged.

In July 1943, as soon as he was legitimately old enough to serve, he enlisted again and took part in the Normandy landings. It was during this time that he was diagnosed as schizophrenic but before treatment could be administered, Neville was taken as a prisoner of war.

Mainly as a result of his illness, Neville refused to co-operate with his captors and spent a great deal of time in solitary confinement; he also received heavy beatings. Neville was in a bad way when he was finally liberated in 1945 but his homecoming was not to be the happy one he had long imagined it would be.

Returning to Dewsbury, he was devastated to learn that one of his brothers had been killed in action serving in Burma. Also his parents had separated and he was still coming to terms with this when he received a message to go to his father's house. On arriving, he found his father had been involved in a street fight and lay dead on the pavement. Standing over his father was a local tough named Cardle who threatened Neville with more of the same if he said anything.

'If you're not careful son, I'll put you in the same place as I have put your father,' Cardle spat at him before being taken into custody. Dennis Neville was one of several witnesses when Cardle stood trial later that year, but whatever hopes he had of seeing his father avenged were shattered when Cardle was acquitted.

Coupled with his schizophrenia, this experience affected Neville to such an extent that he was discharged from the army and after a short stay in a mental hospital was diagnosed as being unfit for further military service.

During the following two years Neville was examined by various doctors, including Dr Leviten, who was consulted with regard to Neville's military pension. Dr Leviten found him to be an emotional wreck. He was distraught at the deaths of both his brother and father, and in particular at the death of his father, for which he blamed Cardle, who lived nearby and whom he still saw often.

Diagnosing Neville as frightened and impulsive, with a resentful and intolerant attitude, Dr Leviten recommended his admittance to a local mental hospital, but after Neville explained his home circumstances, and how he would be leaving his mother and two young sisters alone in the house, it was arranged for him to become an out-patient at Leeds General Hospital.

Seeking a motive for the murder, the prosecution focused on the finding that Marian was pregnant when she was murdered. Leading for the Crown, Mr Harry Hylton-Foster KC told the court that Dennis and Marian had been friends since primary school and they had begun to go out together following his discharge from the army. At this time he found work as a glazier's labourer whilst she worked as a weaver at Britannia Mills.

As their relationship was explained to the court it seemed clear that Marian was keener on Neville than he appeared to be on her. Maybe it was as a result of her intense feelings (she had made it clear that she wanted to marry Neville) that he began to get cold feet and shied away from her to the extent that by the autumn of 1948 he had broken up with her.

Strangely, then, when she told him around this time that she was pregnant by a chap called 'Ronnie', rather than avoid any contact with Marian, Neville seemed to rekindle the relationship and in the following weeks, he too had sexual relations with Marian. It seemed that this was what Marian had planned.

The prosecution claimed that this was the crux of the case: after leaving the dance with Neville, Marian had told him she intended to name him as the father of her child and demanded that he should marry her. They had then gone to the cricket field where after having sexual intercourse again, they had quarrelled: a quarrel which ended when he punched Marian in the face before strangling her.

Summing up the evidence at the end of the two-day trial, Mr Justice Finnemore pointed out to the jury the question of provocation in view of the defence's claim that the crime should be reduced to manslaughter. The defence had pleaded that a reasonable man might well have lost control in these circumstances, but at the judge's guidance they were asked to decide what a 'reasonable man' was.

They needed just one hour to return a guilty verdict. There was a certain amount of shock and surprise in the public gallery as the verdict was returned and Neville was sentenced to death. He neglected to appeal, instead relying on a petition for mercy which received over 7,000 signatures.

On Thursday 2nd June Dennis Neville, a man of misfortune, was hanged at Armley Gaol.

8

'THOSE WRETCHED GANGSTER FILMS'

The Murder of Abraham Levine at Leeds,
November 1949

A cold wind blew down busy Albion Street in Leeds city centre as 52 year old Abraham Harry Levine opened the Albion Watch Depot, his small lock-up jeweller's shop. It was shortly after 10 am on the blustery, wet Wednesday morning of 16th November 1949, and 'Old Abe', as he was sometimes known, had barely raised the shutters and taken his place behind the counter when two young men strolled in. One look at their dress – cheap buttoned-up raincoats and scruffy shoes – suggested to the shrewd shopkeeper that they were unlikely to be big spenders.

'Do you want to buy these?' the older of the two customers asked, placing a number of cheap, service-issue watches on the counter. He gave the goods a cursory glance. 'Sorry, I'm not interested,' Levine replied, pushing them back towards the two youths. Levine was then faced with what he had feared since opening the shop many years earlier. Both customers were now brandishing handguns, and with a sneer they told him to 'hand over the money'.

The till contained the float money of just a few pounds, but Levine wasn't prepared to hand over his money without a struggle. With little regard for his own safety he told them to get out of his shop, and at the same time he came from behind the counter and made a grab at the younger of the two.

The two youths hadn't expected the grey-haired shopkeeper to offer such resistance, seemingly convinced that the sight of the guns would convince him to hand over the money. As Levine grappled with one man, the other raised his weapon and brought it down on the

Gordon Lannen.

Walter Sharpe.

shopkeeper's head. In that same instant his friend fired twice.

The pair panicked, and leaving him slumped against the counter, fled into the street, firing a number of warning shots to deter any would-be heroes from giving chase. Despite his injuries, Mr Levine followed them outside but collapsed in the doorway. Passers-by attempted first aid as he slumped unconscious.

An ambulance took him to Leeds Infirmary where he was placed on the critical list. 'One man hit me on the head, the other shot me,' he managed to tell the police before drifting into a coma.

Superintendent Bowman of the West Riding Murder Squad was put on the case and he assigned all available officers to it. A cordon was thrown around the area and all likely haunts of the criminal underworld were visited without success.

On the following day, Abraham Levine regained consciousness just long enough to dictate a statement giving good descriptions of his attackers. Officers in adjoining counties co-operated in the investigation and a check was made of all traffic leaving Yorkshire, whilst railway police checked all passengers leaving trains originating from Leeds.

On the following evening officers picked up two suspects at Hammersmith who fitted the descriptions of the killers; it had become a murder case when Abraham Levine died from his injuries that

Mr Raymond Hinchcliffe KC.

afternoon. The two were interviewed but were able to prove their innocence.

It was found that the bullets used to kill Levine might have been stolen from a Hunslet gunsmith's shop a week earlier. At the post-mortem carried out at Leeds University Hospital, Professor C. J. Polson found that the bullet which had killed Mr Levine was a .31 cattle-killer bullet but had probably been fired by a .38 revolver. Both this ammunition and the weapon had been stolen from the Hunslet shop.

The trail then crossed the Pennines to Southport where on Friday morning, Detective Inspector Booth and Detective Greenwood of Southport CID spoke to two youths who had been picked up for loitering. Asked for their names and addresses, they told officers they were Walter Sharpe, aged 19, of Brooklands Close, Seaforth, Leeds and 17 year old Gordon Lannen of Throstle Road, Middleton, Leeds.

That they were from Leeds immediately roused suspicions and when they were asked further questions Lannen intimated that they knew something about the murder of the shopkeeper. Questioned separately, he said: 'We did the Leeds job. I was on the job but didn't shoot him. He was shouting and we both hit him to keep him quiet. Then my pal shot him.' Lannen then said that they had burned their raincoats and thrown two revolvers, a Colt and a Webley, along with a quantity of live ammunition, in a river near Southport.

Faced with this confession and the fact that Sharpe had a number of bullets in his jacket pocket, officers were convinced that they had the culprits; the two were returned to Leeds to face trial. The youths, who had been described in the local press as 'gangsters', were brought by train to the city but so hostile was the crowd outside the main police station that they were held in the suburbs before being taken to the remand hearing.

On 9th March 1950, they both appeared at Leeds Assizes before Mr Justice Streatfeild. The trial had a sensational start when Lannen announced that he wished to plead guilty. His counsel, Mr Raymond Hinchcliffe KC, told the judge that the plea was entirely contrary to what he had been advised.

'You don't regard it as the correct plea so far as your advice is concerned?' the judge asked.

'I do not.'

'In that case it would be most undesirable for me to accept the plea. I shall direct a plea of not guilty to be entered.'

Opening the case for the prosecution, Mr G. Russell Vick KC said that the two accused had set out in common adventure to rob Mr Levine. Each had a loaded gun, either to frighten the victim into submission, or to render him incapable of resistance, or to resist arrest. One or both had then struck him over the head with the butt of a revolver and one had shot him in the stomach.

Reference was then made to the statement Lannen had made at Southport, in which he had freely confessed to the murder. The court was told that the hold-up had been the most fantastic failure because as soon as they entered the shop Lannen had panicked. Once the shopkeeper had shown resistance, his only thoughts were to get away from the shop.

Speaking in his own defence, Sharpe made an attempt to state that the shooting was an accident. He said that when Levine had grabbed hold of his panicking friend, Sharpe had tried to intervene and during the struggle a gun had gone off accidentally. He claimed that at first he didn't know that the gun had been fired.

Sharpe had previously admitted stealing the gun, one of four, from a gunsmith's shop. His counsel made a vain attempt to show that Sharpe had been influenced in his actions by watching violent movies at the cinema. He was said to visit the cinema three times a week and had fallen under the influence of 'those wretched gangster films'.

It was a forlorn defence in what his counsel had known from day one was a hopeless case, and on the second day of the trial the jury were invited to consider a verdict. They needed less than 20 minutes to return to find both guilty. Sentence was passed first on Lannen.

'The jury have very properly convicted you on this evidence of a most shocking and disgraceful murder,' the judge told him. 'You come under the protection of the Children and Young Persons Act, and because you are under the age of 18 you cannot suffer the supreme penalty of the law. That act protects even young gangsters. You shall be detained until the King's pleasure be known.'

Lannen was then removed from the dock and a black cap was draped upon the judge's wig as he turned to Sharpe. 'For your part in this most shocking crime it is my duty to pass upon you, young as you are, the sentence which is prescribed by law for this offence.'

Sentence of death was then passed in the usual manner. On Thursday 30th March 1950, Walter Sharpe was hanged at Armley Gaol by Stephen Wade. He was the last person to be hanged in the old execution shed on 'A' wing. Lannen served less than eight years in custody.

It is interesting to note that it was alleged to have been Sharpe's fascination with the violent Hollywood movies, 'those wretched gangster films' as the judge labelled them, which influenced him to commit the murder. Later that year Ealing Films produced the classic melodramatic police film *The Blue Lamp* which featured two young villains robbing a jeweller's shop. Sharp-eyed viewers may notice, in the montage of actual newspaper cuttings shown in the film's introduction, headlines pertaining to the Leeds murder. Thus, in a strange twist, the fictional movies that influenced a real-life murder were followed by a real-life murder case that influenced a fictional movie.

9

A
DEBT SETTLED IN BLOOD

The Murder of Walter Wyld at York,
January 1951

Monday 29th January 1951 was a foul day. Thick snow blanketed almost the whole country, with the bleak north of Yorkshire suffering as much as anywhere. Despite the cold weather police officers were hard at work dragging the ice-covered river Foss at York, looking for the knife that almost 36 hours earlier had been used to commit a brutal murder.

An inquiry had begun on the previous afternoon when sisters Mrs Raby and Mrs Clark, who lived either side of 199 Huntington Road, York, the home of 72 year old widower Walter Wyld, became concerned for their neighbour's health. Unusually, the curtains were still drawn at 1 pm, and after getting no reply to their persistent knocking, Mrs Raby took the spare key and along with her nephew Eric Clark, entered the house.

With the heavy drapes still closed they made their way inside in almost total darkness until Eric located the lightswitch. When it was switched on they found Walter Wyld stretched out on the kitchen floor. The old man was lying on his back, his arms bound with flex, and from the bloodstains that covered his chest it appeared he had been stabbed several times.

Police officers were quickly at the scene under the command of Inspector George Garbutt of York City Police CID. It seemed clear that robbery was the motive; the man's trouser pockets had been turned out and the furniture in the living room was disturbed in such a way as to suggest both that there had been a struggle and that someone had been looking for something.

58

The inspector noticed that there appeared to be no sign of a forced entry, which suggested that the victim had allowed the killer to enter the house, in turn suggesting that he might well be an acquaintance. This was not surprising as Walter Wyld was a very popular and well known figure in the area. A former rugby league footballer, he had devoted most of his spare time to his favourite rugby football team, York, and for the last 25 years he had served as both gateman and steward at the club.

A check on his movements on the previous evening found that he had enjoyed a post-match whist drive in the social club at York Rugby League ground on Wiggington Road. He had left the club at 9.45 pm and walked to the bus stop, where he chatted with an old friend before he caught the bus alone to Huntington Road, a journey of less than five minutes. No witnesses could be found who had seen him after he boarded the bus.

Having arranged for the body to be transferred to a local hospital, the inspector called for the assistance of Scotland Yard, and whilst awaiting their arrival he searched the house for any clues as to why the old man had been killed. Under the stairs was an ancient gas stove, and inside, behind an old gas mask, was a tin containing £73.

The post-mortem, carried out at the hospital by Home Office pathologist Dr David Price, revealed that Wyld had been the subject of a vicious attack. He had suffered head injuries, most likely following a fall, but the cause of death was three stab wounds made with a long thin knife, one of which had entered the body near the spine to a depth of seven inches. The cuts to the hands told how the old man had fought to the last to wrestle the blade away from the killer.

On the following afternoon Detective Superintendent Jack Capstick and Detective Sergeant Joe Plater arrived from London to take over the investigation. Going over the few clues, Capstick quickly came to the conclusion that the killer was not a 'professional thief', reasoning that even the dumbest crook would not have failed to have found the money under the stairs. Also, the neighbours, keeping an ever-watchful eye on the elderly neighbour, would have heard signs of trouble if a stranger or an intruder had committed the crime. In any case, with the key still in the door and no sign of forced entry, the idea of a break-in had already been discarded.

Over the next few days, as waste ground close to Huntington Road was searched for the murder weapon and any other clues, police officers interviewed over 3,000 inhabitants. Hardly anyone had a bad

John Dand.

word to say about Walter Wyld; but more importantly, several reported that the old man often lent them sums of money, anything ranging from a few shillings to several pounds.

From a bundle of letters found in the kitchen drawer it seemed that Wyld ran a very small-time loan business, his clients predominantly being friends and neighbours and he charged little if any interest. Amongst the letters was one which caught the attention of Superintendent Capstick. It was dated 9th January 1951, and postmarked Kirkcaldy, Fife. It read:

Dear Walter,
I have just come in and got your letter. I was very pleased to hear from you until I read about the money. I hope you will remember that I paid you that money off the third pay I drew from Rowntrees. I was grateful for the loan when I got it, Walter, and I am very sorry you think I left without paying. I had to come home in a hurry because my mother had an accident or else I would have been to see you. Jock is back in York now, so whenever I get his address I will tell him to come to see you.
Yours sincerely
I. Dand (Mrs)

This suggested to Capstick a possible motive: an unpaid debt is as good as any reason for murder. Inquiries were made and it was found that the Dand family once lived a few doors away from Walter Wyld in Huntington Road, and by all accounts they had been good friends. They later moved across the city but remained friends. In November 1950 the family had returned to their native Kirkcaldy, but on 7th January 1951, John Dand returned to York, leaving behind his wife and family.

Capstick found that Dand was living at lodgings on Burlington Avenue, in the Tang Hall district, and he asked Inspector Garbutt to invite Dand to accompany him to the murder headquarters at York Central police station. At 6 pm, on Wednesday 31st January, four days after the murder, Capstick saw 32 year old John 'Jock' Dand for the first time. Dand was a former soldier with an impressive military record. During the war he had fought bravely and had been awarded the Military Medal. It was with great reluctance that Dand had left the army: he was invalided out with duodenal ulcers, and although he had found work as a press operator, he still spent much of his time socialising with servicemen in the mess club at the local Fulford Barracks.

Asked when he had last seen Walter Wyld, Dand spoke in a strong

Scots accent: 'About Monday 8th January. I called at his house, we had a chat in the kitchen, and I gave him £3 I had borrowed from him.'

'I want to check your movements after 10 pm on Saturday 27th January,' Capstick asked, to which Dand replied firmly: 'I can prove I did not kill him.'

Inviting him to do just that, Capstick asked if he had any objection to the clothes he wore that night being sent for forensic examination. Dand said that he had only one suit and he was willing to let the police have it.

In the statement Dand made that night, the former soldier said that he had spent the evening drinking in various pubs in York in the company of two friends: Sergeant McIrvine from Fulford Barracks, and fellow Scot Ted Hutton. He left them at about 10.45 pm to return to his lodgings. After signing the statement, he accompanied the detectives back to his lodgings to hand over his clothes. Capstick noted that Dand chainsmoked throughout the interview.

Back at Burlington Avenue, the officers took possession of items of clothing and a number of letters found in the bedside drawer. One, from Dand's wife, was a rebuke to him for not repaying the loan to Walter Wyld; the other was from the victim stating that he had been trying to find Dand and also asking for repayment as soon as possible.

A third letter was found. Addressed to Mrs Dand, it read:

> Your letter to hand this morning, and very pleased to hear from you. I think there is a misunderstanding somewhere. I am quite aware you paid me the £3 I lent you. About three weeks after you went to St Paul's Square, Jock came to see me and I lent him another £3 which has not been repaid, so I think that clears you? Did you not know that? I am sorry if you did not know. Anyhow, he may come to see you and explain . . .

It was signed Walter Wyld. Capstick, whilst checking Dand's statement, decided to take a close look into his spending habits over the recent weeks. Discreet inquiries soon revealed that Dand was spending more than he could have earned in the factory, but he was also in debt to a number of friends.

More importantly, checks into Dand's statement regarding his movements on the night of the murder found discrepancies concerning the time at which Dand said he parted from his friends. His drinking companions told the detectives that they had been with Jock Dand only until 9.20 pm, a good hour or so earlier than he had said. Dand had told his friends: 'I've got to go to keep an important date. I'm meeting a girl who is going to get me a job. I'll come back again if I have time.' Dand failed to return and there were no reported sightings of him that night, although his landlady told police that she heard him go to bed at around midnight.

There was also strong forensic evidence linking Dand with the crime. Mr Lewis Charles Nickolls, director of the forensic science laboratory at Wakefield, reported that he had found traces of blood on the clothes Dand had submitted for examination. The blood was group 'A', the same as that of the dead man, while Dand's own blood group was 'O'.

On Saturday afternoon, 3rd February, one week after the murder, Superintendent Capstick, in the company of Sergeant Plater and Inspector Wild of York CID, called at Burlington Avenue and found Dand still in bed. He was again asked to account for his movements on the night of the murder; after a wash and shave, Dand accompanied them back to the police station.

'We have checked your statement and found that you have told us a pack of lies,' Capstick said. Told that Sergeant McIrvine had made a statement to the effect that Dand had left him and Hutton much earlier than he had told them, Dand's hard expression didn't change. He looked Capstick in the eye and declared: 'Yes, that's right. I'll tell you the truth.'

Capstick waited. For ten minutes the hunter and his prey sat face to face in silence. Finally, Dand spoke. Slowly. 'I left my pals and picked up a woman who was walking away from the Elephant and Castle. We went on the river bank where we were intimate. Later I walked back to my lodgings, arriving there about 11.30 pm.'

Asked to account for the blood on his raincoat and trousers, Dand again lapsed into silence for a few minutes before stating that it must have come from the woman. 'Tell me her name and where I can find her,' Capstick said.

Further silence prevailed, during which time an incident occurred that would play a prominent part when the case came to court. Throughout the interview there had been three detectives facing the suspect. During this last period of silence, Inspector Wild of York CID left the room to speak to other officers, leaving Dand alone with the Scotland Yard men.

Capstick told him he disbelieved his story. Dand then lowered his head, covered his eyes with his hands and spoke in almost a whisper: 'I admit that we had a row about money. It was an accident and I left him there.'

He was about to continue when the officers had to stop him and give the standard caution that anything he said would be taken down in evidence.

Inspector Wild then re-entered and Dand dictated a statement that described how he had spent the night in various pubs, then picked up a woman before returning to his lodgings. The statement ended with the bold declaration: 'I deny going to Walter Wyld's house on the night he was murdered. There is nothing more I can say.'

Despite the retraction, Inspector Wild, convinced that Dand was the man who had killed Walter Wyld, formally charged him with murder.

Dand's trial opened before Mr Justice Gorman at Leeds Assizes on 23rd April, in the same town hall building where the infamous Charlie Peace and numerous other criminals had stood trial in the past. Dand was defended by Mr H. R. Shepherd KC, one of the shrewdest defence counsel of the day.

The case against Dand was substantial: notwithstanding the confession made to Capstick, there was much evidence against the prisoner, including forensic clues and the discredited alibi he had offered when first questioned.

As the trial developed the defence focused on the 'alleged' confession and intimated that it seemed strange that this had come when Dand was left in the company of the two Scotland Yard officers. Dand's counsel suggested that this may have been bullied out of the prisoner.

When the case was summed up, the facts seemed clear. Dand owed Walter Wyld a sum of money. On the night of 27th January he had called at the house and they had quarrelled over the debt and following this, Dand had stabbed the old man to death. The paltry debt, which Dand settled in blood, was just £3.

Retiring for a little over an hour, the jury found Dand guilty as charged and he was sentenced to death. At the end of May, his appeal was refused and he returned to await execution.

The gallows at Armley Gaol were being modernised during this period and as a result Dand was transferred to Manchester's Strangeways Gaol; the date set for his execution was Tuesday 12th June 1951.

Albert Pierrepoint and assistant Harry Allen were appointed to carry out the sentence. Like the accused, Allen had grown up in Kirkcaldy, but the two men were unknown to each other. Allen noted in his diary that Dand smoked continually right up to the time he was led to the drop, and that even when the straps were fastened around his arms he asked for a last cigarette. Ten seconds later, Walter Wyld was avenged.

10

BEYOND
REASONABLE DOUBT?

The Murders of Inspector Duncan Fraser and Constable
Arthur Gordon Jagger at Kirkheaton,
July 1951

Detectives in the West Riding Police
Force had long suspected that Alfred Moore had a secret pastime.
Although he earned a reasonable income as a poultry farmer at his
secluded home at Whinney Close Farm, Kirkheaton, a few miles from
Huddersfield, they believed that he was also a skilled burglar
responsible for over a hundred unsolved crimes. This assumption
was based on the fact that Moore and his family were known to be
living above his income as a simple poultry farmer: his children
travelled daily by taxi to an expensive private school, and his
farmhouse was stocked with furniture and artefacts well beyond the
means of a normal Yorkshire farmer.

It was because of his suspected past misdemeanours that Moore
came to the attention of detectives faced with a mountain of unsolved
crimes in the summer of 1951. During the war, Moore had decided that
he had no wish to fight for King and country and had duly absconded
from his unit. He had kept away from the authorities until well after
hostilities had ended, whereupon he was charged with an offence
alleged to have been committed in 1943.

On 30th May 1947, he stood accused of a robbery committed nearly
four years earlier, but when the case came to trial there was no
evidence to convict Moore and he was acquitted. However, the press
coverage of the trial had come to the attention of the military police and
when he was formally discharged at Leeds Assizes his new-found

The entrance to Whinney Close Farm, Kirkheaton, as it looks today.

freedom was soon tempered; he was immediately arrested and charged with desertion. He put up a fierce struggle before being subdued and taken into custody.

It was a matter of routine that when Moore was charged, his 'mug-shot' photograph was taken and put in his file, and it was this photograph that was to play a vital role in events that took place four years later.

Detective Inspector Duncan Fraser, known as 'Sandy' to his colleagues, was the head of Huddersfield CID, and at 45 years old, had over 22 years' service. For the last couple of years he had become increasingly frustrated by the mounting number of unsolved burglaries and break-ins at local mills and offices. Amongst the main suspects was Alfred Moore, and Fraser had made it his business to clear up some of the unsolved crimes before his forthcoming retirement.

During the early part of the summer of 1951, Moore was kept under observation but without arousing his suspicions. On the night of Saturday 14th July, Chief Inspector Jenkins, believing that Moore was out on a job, formed a ten-man team that included Fraser and a number of constables, and set a trap to catch a thief. They had watched the goings-on at Whinney Close Farm and felt sure that if a cordon was

The mug-shot of Alfred Moore which may
have led to his conviction.

Alfred Moore in 1951.

thrown around the farm when Moore was out, then on his return he
would be caught red-handed.

It was a simple plan and when darkness had fallen it was put into
operation. The men, who had been shown the 'mug-shot' photograph
of Moore to aid recognition, were posted in pairs and each was
equipped with a pair of binoculars, a torch and a police whistle. The
plan was that from 11.45 pm that night, all roads to the farm were
effectively sealed off and no one could leave or gain entrance without
being spotted.

Simple as it was, the plan failed. Shortly before 2 am, five shots rang
out across the field. Police Constable Sellick rushed to where he
thought the shots had originated and found both Inspector Fraser and
Constable Gordon Jagger lying shot on the grass, about 80 yards apart
and less than 350 yards from the house.

With their cover broken, police lights flashed and assistance was
called for. It was found that Inspector Fraser had died from his injuries.
Constable Jagger lay unconscious, bleeding heavily from gunshot
wounds to the stomach. They were removed to Huddersfield Infirmary

Detective Inspector Duncan Fraser.

where valiant attempts were made to save the wounded officer.

Hordes of police now converged on the farmhouse and although a light was seen to glow in a bedroom window for a few minutes after the

PC Arthur Gordon Jagger.

sound of gunshots, there was no further activity until shortly before 5 am when smoke began to billow from a chimney. The chimney smoked intermittently for some 15 minutes, as if someone was adding combustible material to the fire.

Detective Superintendent George Metcalfe, the CID chief who had arrived with armed officers to take over the investigation, now decided to approach the farmhouse shouting: 'Come out, we are police officers.

Moore's wife answered the door and asked what they wanted. Told they wanted to speak to her husband, she asked them why; and when Moore came to the door dressed in a pair of flannel trousers and wearing Wellington boots, he was placed under arrest.

Moore denied the charge of shooting two police officers in Cockley Hill fields that morning. He showed the officer the only gun he owned, a shotgun, and it was taken away for forensic examination. Moore was then taken into custody.

As Moore was held in the police cells, doctors fought in vain to save the life of Constable Jagger. He was given a blood transfusion and as he clung on to life, Metcalfe questioned his prisoner.

Moore told him that he had walked his brother part-way home and had returned to his farm at around 11.35 pm:

'I went to bed at about 12 o'clock . . . I never got up again . . .'

'What about the smoke seen coming from your chimney?' Metcalfe asked.

'If you must know, I got up to burn some rubbish. I'm not saying any more. I want time to think . . . I am in an awful spot. I think I'll have a solicitor.'

A search of the fields and farmhouse had failed to locate the murder weapon and with nothing to prove directly that Moore had carried out the shootings, Metcalfe organised an identity parade to be held before the dying constable. Eight men of similar height and build to Moore were gathered up and paraded before Jagger. Scanning the line-up, the constable immediately pointed out Moore.

The police could now act and Metcalfe charged Moore with the murder of Inspector Fraser.

'How could it be me? I have told you, I was in bed,' he persisted.

A short time later, an emergency courtroom was set up in a private ward at the hospital, where Constable Jagger gave evidence for the last time: 'I first saw the accused at 2 am on 15th July. He was walking towards his home. As I got near to him, he must have heard my feet in the grass and dashed under a hedge. I said "Hello" and shouted.

'He said "I thought it was a cow." I shone my torch in his face and took hold of his left arm. I saw his face clearly in the light of the torch. As I took hold of the accused's left arm Mr Fraser approached and shone his torch into the accused's face. "Are you Moore?" "Yes," he replied.

'Mr Fraser said: "We are police officers and you are coming with us." He said "No sir. Oh, no sir."

'As soon as the accused said that he whipped his hand, his right hand, out of his overcoat pocket and shot me and Mr Fraser . . .'

In the early hours of the following morning, the case against Moore became one of double murder.

Alfred Moore stood trial before Mr Justice Pearson shortly before Christmas 1951. In the period after his arrest police had combed the farmhouse looking for the murder weapon and any other firm evidence linking him with the murders, but without success. What they did find, though, was a tremendous amount of stolen property connecting him with many of the unsolved burglaries that littered the desk of Inspector Fraser, the man whom he was now charged with murdering.

Opening for the Crown, Mr Raymond Hinchcliffe KC told the court that a callous murder had been committed and that the prosecution submitted that the prisoner in the dock was the man responsible. The crux of their case stemmed from the deathbed identification parade in which the mortally wounded PC Jagger had pointed the finger at Moore as the man who had shot him.

Moore's defence counsel, Mr Hylton-Foster KC, pointed to the lack of real evidence against the accused. He asked where the murder weapon was. Moore had only one gun at the farm, a shotgun, which had been forensically proved not to be the murder weapon. If Moore had, as the Crown claimed, returned home from committing a crime and shot dead the two officers, then surely the gun must either be in the house or have been discarded on his land as he made his way home. Army officers with metal detectors had meticulously searched the surrounding area but had failed to uncover any such weapon.

'Had you anything to do with the shootings?' his counsel asked.

'No,' Moore replied.

'Do you know who shot them?'

'I have no idea.'

'On that night were you involved in any crime at all?'

'No,' Moore said.

He claimed that he had walked his brother home and returned at around 11.45 pm.

Closing his case, Mr Hinchcliffe referred back to the identification parade in which Moore had been pointed out by Constable Jagger.

'You were given the opportunity to cross-examine him?'

'Yes,' Moore replied.

'Was the question put "Are you sure?"?'

'It was, sir.'

'And the answer was "I am quite sure"?'

'Yes.'

With that, Hinchcliffe sat down dramatically. He later asked the jury to consider how Moore could have returned to the farm at the time he claimed, when the police cordon had already been put into position. This was countered easily by the defence, who explained that with the officers being as far apart as they were, Moore, who knew the land well enough to walk it in the dark, had merely bypassed them and walked home unaware that a cordon was in position.

The jury needed less than an hour to return a guilty verdict and Moore was sentenced to be hanged.

'I am not guilty,' he cried out after the verdict was delivered.

There was little sympathy for the convicted police-killer and his appeal failed. Lord Goddard, who presided over the appeal, pointed again to the evidence of PC Jagger's dying declaration.

On the morning of Wednesday 6th February 1952, Alfred Moore was hanged. Public interest in his execution was overshadowed in that day's newspapers by the death of King George VI, who passed away a few hours before Moore walked to the gallows.

Was Alfred Moore a callous double murderer or the victim of a wrongful identification? Certainly the evidence, as it was reported both at the time and since, suggests that the conviction may have been unsafe.

In the book *Scales of Justice*, Fenton Bresler puts forward a theory, which, after researching the case, I believe stands up to scrutiny. Bresler suggests that the real killer may have been a 'friend' of Alfred Moore, perhaps a fence calling at the house to do some 'business', who inadvertently stumbled into the police cordon.

Asked if he was Moore, the man replied that he was, being unlikely to reveal his own name. On the assumption that this man was carrying a gun, he could then have shot the two men and instead of approaching the farmhouse, merely retraced his steps away from the cordon.

Whilst it may be unfair to discredit the evidence of the dying man, the fact is that he had just come round from major surgery, and had been shown the 'mug-shot' photograph of Moore prior to forming the cordon. It is therefore possible that although he spoke in good faith, he wrongly identified Alfred Moore as the killer.

Moore protested his innocence to the last. On the night before his execution he continued his protestations in between crying out his wife's name. Bresler claims that whilst researching his book, he spoke to locals who remember the shootings. More than one said that Moore was innocent and that they knew the real identity of the killer.

Perhaps Alfred Moore did kill two police officers on that summer's night; however, on the evidence as it was reported both at the time and since, the question must be asked: was it 'beyond reasonable doubt'?

11

A
SON'S DISHONOUR

The Murder of William Henry Robinson at Wakefield,
August 1957

It was a building society manager's suspicions that started the routine police investigation. On Monday 12th August 1957, a young man had entered the Wakefield branch of the Halifax Building Society and told the Chief Clerk, Mr Ingrams, that his father wished to have some money transferred from his account to the son's. The man said that his father was to go into an old people's home at Hull and as his care was being partly funded by the corporation, the father needed to diversify his savings to qualify for assistance.

He produced two documents purporting to be signed by his father that asked for the transfer. The man gave an address at Alpha Terrace, Hull, and asked for any further correspondence to be sent there. The letters were signed William Henry Robinson, but when the clerk compared them against a sample signature at the office he became suspicious and refused the transaction. He did, however, send out a further form to be signed by the father and this was dispatched later that day.

On the following Friday, the same young man called at the Hull branch and asked for £30 to be transferred to his account. Again he was refused. On the next morning he was back at the Wakefield branch, this time with a letter signed 'Laurence Avery' and an address in Hull where the father was supposed to be staying. Also presented was a letter signed by a Dr O'Neill claiming that the old man's signature had changed since he had injured his hand in a fall. Still not convinced by the claims, the clerk again refused the transaction; moreover, he now became suspicious that a fraud might be being perpetrated. When a

William Henry Robinson.

further attempt to extract money was made a few days later, the clerk again refused and this time contacted the police.

The suspected fraud was handled by Detective Inspector Kenneth Oakley and Detective Constable Alan Kirk. Both were experienced in this type of investigation and a few days after the last attempted withdrawal, they called at a house on Denby Dale Road, Wakefield, and spoke to the young man who had made a number of failed attempts to withdraw money.

Two things immediately struck the officers as the front door opened. The first was that 20 year old George Frederick Robinson-Brannon was clearly a homosexual; the second was a revolting smell emanating from the house. The two officers questioned the occupier and though he tried to appear normal and relaxed, acting in a businesslike way, his manner was clearly effeminate and he tended to flounce and flutter around as they studied him.

Straight to the point, the officers asked him why he was trying to obtain money from his father's account. Giving them a plausible reason, Robinson-Brannon said that his elderly father was ill, and unable to get to the building society himself.

'The rent still has to be paid you know,' he told the detectives, adding that he had also to find money for food.

'You told the manager that your father is in Hull. Is that correct?' Oakley asked him.

'No!' the young man replied. 'The manager must have misunderstood. He is in Heckmondwike.'

The officers asked Robinson-Brannon to accompany them to the station while they made further inquiries. Neighbours told them that the old man had not been seen since early August after he had been released from hospital. George was the only son still at home, and had lived there with his father following the death of their mother in 1953. Several neighbours also commented on the strange smell that appeared to come from the house in recent weeks.

At that first visit the officers had made a cursory search of the house and noticed in an upstairs bedroom a bucket of faeces. Could this have been the cause of the unpleasant stench? Or had it been placed there to disguise something more sinister? More disturbingly, they learned that Robinson-Brannon had told varying accounts of what had happened to his father. To one pawnshop-keeper he said that his father was in an old people's home, to another he said that the old man had died and showed a will as proof.

Firemen removing the body of William Henry Robinson from his home in Denby Dale Road, Wakefield.

DC Kirk was given the task of locating the home in Heckmondwike and after a futile search he returned to Wakefield with the news that it did not exist. So where was the old man? The police decided to make a thorough search of the house on Denby Dale Road. Despite the bucket having been removed from the bedroom, the stench still persisted and it was decided to make a top-to-bottom examination of the house to find the cause of the smell.

Over four tons of coal was shifted from the cellar but revealed nothing. Likewise, nothing untoward was found downstairs; the smell seemed to emanate from the bedroom, in particular from the old Victorian wardrobe that stood in an alcove. This was empty, but Kirk arranged for it to be taken outside, and when it was removed something suspicious was revealed.

The wardrobe had been placed in front of a closet door – a door that was now nailed shut – and stuffed around the gaps were a number of rags. The door was forced open and out fell a maggot-ridden body. The whereabouts of William Henry Robinson had been located.

Pathologist Dr David Price was called to the scene. The state of the body was such that it was impossible to undertake more than a brief examination. Because of the fragile nature of the corpse, it was decided not to try to remove it down the narrow staircase; instead police arranged for the local fire brigade, using a sling and ropes, to hoist it from the bedroom window.

Back at the police station, Robinson-Brannon was informed that the body of his father had been located and he broke down, claiming the old man's death had been an accident. 'I never intended to harm my father,' he sobbed as he finished making a statement. 'I have been going through a living hell.'

On Tuesday 11th December 1957, he stood before Mr Justice Streatfeild at Leeds Assizes, charged with patricide.

Mr Rudolph Lyons QC, prosecuting, opened his case by stating that the accused and his father had been the sole occupants of the house for four years and there had been friction between them after the father discovered that his son had forged his signature on some saving certificates that he had cashed in. This had been the second time George had tried to swindle his father in this way.

George knew that his father had over £500 invested in the building society, money he knew he had planned to divide between George and his half-brother. Lyons said that he intended to show that the accused regarded his father as nothing more than a barrier between himself and that money.

'Rarely, if ever, has a jury had the misfortune to listen to so dreadful a story of a son's dishonour of his father and the desecration of his memory,' he told the court. He said that sometime between 6th and 15th August 1957, the accused had killed his father, bundling his body into the closet and then nailing it shut. He then stuffed rags into the gap between the door and the frame and placed the wardrobe in front of the door. Robinson-Brannon had then slept in that same room for over three weeks while he plotted a scheme to get at the money. The father was described as a gentle and frail old man, whose death had been both deliberate and premeditated.

The post-mortem had revealed the cause of death as manual strangulation, despite a leather belt having been found fastened around the man's neck. Cross-examined by Mr J. F. Drabble QC, the accused's counsel, Dr Price stood firm in his belief that the cause of death was nothing other than a deliberate act of strangulation; the damage to both the voicebox and the hyoid bone convinced the pathologist that death had been intentional.

Challenging the claims that the victim was a frail and gentle old man, counsel called a number of witnesses to claim that he was cantankerous and had a foul temper, a trait that might suggest that there could be some justification in the accused quarrelling and perhaps struggling with his father.

Robinson-Brannon took the stand and spoke in his own defence. Dressed in a sombre dark suit, he told the court that he had been indecently assaulted as a youth and this experience had led him to his tendencies. Initially he had fought against these and two years before the alleged murder he had got a girl pregnant. His father had refused to allow him to marry her, and later that year he accused his son of having a homosexual relationship in the house with a friend called 'Laurie'.

They had quarrelled and despite his son denying the accusations, the father let loose a tirade of abuse, calling him all sorts of names and even blaming him for the death of his mother by saying his deviant behaviour had broken her heart.

Robinson-Brannon said that on the night of the murder he had wanted to go out but his father had tried to stop him, saying he couldn't go out drinking until he had paid his board of £3. 5s. The accused had recently left his job as a copy typist and this was another reason for his father's anger. The two had quarrelled and when George tried to leave, his father got out a leather strap and struck him with it.

Describing how his father had met his death, the accused sobbed and said: 'I knocked it out of his hand and hit him across the head. He fell and struck his head on a chair. I left the house and when I returned he was still there. I checked his breathing and he seemed to be dead. I put a piece of rope around his waist and a leather belt around his neck and dragged him upstairs. I took his watch and the money from his pockets before placing him in the closet.'

Challenging this account, which suggested nothing more than accidental death in self-defence, the Crown claimed that on that same night he had been seen in pubs wearing his father's watch and chain and had later invited friends back to the house – hardly the behaviour of someone who had accidentally killed his father and was panicking about what to do.

Closing the defence's case, Robinson-Brannon's counsel asked the jury to disregard the Crown's story as a 'melodramatic account' and to find the accused guilty of manslaughter: 'This was not a premeditated attack. It was a sudden killing done in the heat of the moment.'

The jury took less than two hours to find him guilty of wilful murder. The judge, in passing sentence, said it was a sordid and dreadful case and that the accused was a self-confessed homosexual and forger, a man who would lie with impunity and who, having taken his father's life, had no scruples about stealing every penny the old man owned.

George Robinson-Brannon collapsed as sentence was passed and had to be escorted from the dock to begin his sentence of life imprisonment.

12

IN
THE FURTHERANCE OF THEFT

The Murder of Richard Turner at Lepton,
September 1958

Like his father before him, Richard Turner was employed as a manager with the Co-operative Society. Whereas his father had managed a branch at Highburton, Richard, or Dick as he was known to his friends, had, after ten years' service, graduated from counter-hand to become manager at the Cowms branch on Station Road, Lepton.

Thirty-eight year old Turner was a conscientious manager and as there had been a spate of robberies on this and similar stores in recent months, including one at the Cowms store itself in the spring of 1957, he was always most careful to make sure the shop was locked up and the takings were in the safe. Indeed, only a week earlier another unsuccessful attempt had been made to break into the Cowms store.

It was almost a matter of routine for Turner, once he had eaten his supper, to leave his home at Spa Terrace, Lepton, and check all was well at the shop. It was also not unusual for him to have an evening drink in the Ashfield Liberal Club 30 yards from the store. On leaving the club he would then make a quick check at the store before returning home.

Tuesday 30th September 1958 had been half-day closing in Lepton and that night, as was his custom, once the family had taken supper, Turner drove the short distance to the shop to check that all was well. Kathleen Turner became anxious when her husband failed to return home at the usual time that Tuesday night and eventually she called at the store. Her husband's car was parked outside; there was a light on, but the door was locked and no one answered when she knocked.

The Cowms store where the body was found is now a Spar shop.

Mrs Turner then called at the Liberal Club and approached a group of men who were leaving. She spoke to one of her husband's friends, Jack Howe, who agreed to accompany her back to the store. Outside they were joined by further friends, including a couple who lived adjacent to the shop. The crowd began to bang on the window trying to attract attention from anyone inside, but without success.

Remembering that her husband sometimes kept a spare set of keys at home, Kathleen, accompanied by Howe, went back to Spa Terrace, but finding no sign of the keys, they decided to call for the assistant manager, Herbert Whittle. One of those outside the shop noticed that Dick Turner had left his keys in the ignition, so he used his car to go and fetch Mr Whittle; they returned at 11.40 pm.

The two men entered the shop. Whittle searched downstairs whilst Michael Jessop searched upstairs. Jessop returned moments later looking very shaken. Realising something was wrong, Mrs Turner hurried into the shop, and on climbing the stairs she saw the body of her husband lying outside the office. His head was covered with blood and he was obviously dead. Mrs Turner was taken out of the shop whilst the police and an ambulance were called.

Detective Superintendent Foster, head of the Huddersfield Division

Ernest Raymond Jones.

of the West Riding Police, launched a murder inquiry. He was met at the scene by Detective Inspector Edward Lumb of the divisional CID. On the following morning the team was joined by Detective Chief Superintendent George Metcalfe, head of the West Riding CID, who several years earlier had helped send police-killer Alfred Moore to the gallows (see Chapter 10).

One of the first items on the agenda was to check the place for fingerprints. This was to be a massive job, given the nature of the business, but they concentrated on the rear window where an attempt to force entry had been made.

A number of clues were found at the store. It seemed that the killer had left a heel print in the storeroom and investigations found that it had been made by an 'Avon heel', a rubber heel that left a distinctive pattern of several small circles. It was quite an unusual heel, and bootmakers in the area were questioned to see if they could offer any leads. Also found at the scene was a stocking which under a microscope yielded a number of unusual green fibres.

A post-mortem on the murdered man found that he had died as a result of a fractured skull and it appeared that he had been struck with a blunt instrument which had broken the skull in five places.

Chief Superintendent Metcalfe had also noticed that the killer had left a box near the counter filled with cigarettes and other easy-to-sell items such as hosiery and items of clothing, to the value of nearly £40. Missing from the safe was £76 in small notes and a large amount of change. It was reasoned that Mr Turner must have disturbed someone in the store and that he had been bludgeoned either to prevent him identifying the thief or to stop him escaping.

Metcalfe turned his attention back to the break-in and looked at the recent spate of similar crimes to see if he could come up with any leads. His officers were sent to interview anyone in the area who had been convicted of similar crimes and on 2nd October they called at a house in Temperance Street, Wyke, Bradford, and spoke to Ernest Raymond Jones.

Jones was a 39 year old Welshman from Newton, Monmouthshire, who had been released from Armley Gaol earlier that year after serving a sentence for breaking into a Co-op store at Goldthorpe, near Doncaster. Jones was one of a gang who stole over £1,500 pounds from the store and at the West Riding quarter sessions in the autumn of 1957 he was sentenced to 12 months' imprisonment.

When detectives interviewed Jones regarding the break-in at Lepton he denied any knowledge of it and claimed that he had been at home with his wife on that Tuesday night watching television. Satisfied with this account for the time being, police inquiries were concentrated elsewhere, but on the following Sunday, Detective Chief Inspector Joe

Glendinning called again at the house on Temperance Street and asked Jones further questions. The detective told Jones he had evidence that suggested his previous story was untrue and that witnesses had seen him in Huddersfield on the evening of the murder.

This time Jones changed his story and admitted that he had been in Huddersfield; he then went on to give a different account of his movements. Now he told police that he had travelled into Huddersfield with his wife on the afternoon of 30th September, and after spending some time in a bookmaker's shop, he had had tea at Booth's café, then a drink at the Kirkgate Inn. Jones claimed that he had left the inn at 9 pm and walked the streets for an hour or so, and during this time he had spotted a policewoman as he sheltered from the rain opposite the market place. After taking a statement, the officers left.

Eight days after the murder, officers again called at Jones's house and this time he was taken into custody. He was told that parts of his statement did not add up, in particular the story about seeing a policewoman: investigations had found that there was no woman PC on duty in that part of town at the time Jones claimed.

As Jones was being questioned at the station a search was made of his house, where a number of valuable clues linking him to the murder were found. Amongst the clues was a stocking matching the one found in the store. More importantly, the green fibres on the stocking found at the scene of the murder matched those found on coconut matting in the kitchen at Jones's house.

Also found in a dustbin at the house were the ashes of the kitchen fire, which contained the remnants of a pair of boots. These were taken to the North Eastern Forensic Laboratory at Harrogate where they were found to have had an 'Avon heel' which matched the imprint from the Lepton store. Further incriminating evidence was found in samples of paint from Jones's jacket pocket which matched the scrapings from the window where the intruder had gained entry.

In due course, Ernest Raymond Jones stood trial before Mr Justice Hinchcliffe at Leeds Assizes, a courtroom to which Jones was no stranger. Opening the case against him, Mr Geoffrey Veal QC said that Jones was being charged with capital murder, that is murder in the course or furtherance of theft, and that there was 'well nigh overwhelming evidence to prove that Jones was the intruder who had killed the store manager on 30th September'.

Dr David Price, the Home Office pathologist, was called to say that his examination had found that Mr Turner had died as a result of a blow to the head. Crown counsel claimed that a witness would be called who had spoken to Jones on the day prior to the murder; Jones had claimed he was short of money and had offered to sell the witness a large quantity of cigarettes. The cigarettes, the counsel claimed, were one of the reasons Jones had chosen to rob the store.

The landlady at the house where Jones lived with his wife had told police that on the morning after the murder, she had seen Mrs Jones counting a large amount of silver coins which she had then taken to be changed into notes. Jones had also told her to buy him some new boots and he had then burned his old pair on the kitchen fire.

One of the most damning testimonies had come from Jones himself when he had told a police constable after his arrest that 'it is too late for my solicitor to do anything for me now . . . I was there. I just shoved him.' Jones had maintained throughout that he had merely pushed Mr Turner when he was confronted by him at the top of the stairs and he had only done so to escape. He denied striking him with his fist, even though a witness told police she had overheard Jones telling his wife at the police station that he only given him a 'rabbit punch' to the head.

Bearing in mind the gravity of the charge, which carried the death penalty if the accused was convicted, his counsel, Mr Bernard Gillis QC, was faced with a hard task when he opened the defence on the third day of the trial. The evidence clearly put Jones in the store at the time of the 'murder', and so Mr Gillis offered the defence of manslaughter, stating that at no time did Jones intend to injure the victim, and that although he had pushed Turner, this was only to make good his escape. He strongly rejected the Crown's suggestion that Jones had struck the manager with any kind of instrument, asserting that he had merely given him a shove.

Another key point made by the defence concerned the wording of the charge. One category of capital murder was deemed to be a 'murder committed in the furtherance of theft' and Gillis claimed that technically the theft had only been completed if Jones was ready to leave the store. The implication was that if at worst he was guilty of murder, it would be non-capital murder, which would warrant only a prison sentence.

In the late afternoon of Wednesday 10th December 1958, the three-day trial ended with the jury returning a guilty verdict. Mr Justice Hinchcliffe then sentenced Jones to death. His wife burst into tears as he was led from the dock.

An appeal was launched on Jones's behalf on the basis that the murder had not been committed in the furtherance of theft, but at the appeal court in January 1959 the Lord Chief Justice dismissed the appeal by stating that 'if a burglar is interrupted and if he murders in order to get away it is still murder in the furtherance of theft'. Jones was returned to the death cell at Armley to await execution. On 10th February 1959, Ernest Jones was hanged.

There is an interesting footnote to this case. In the days of capital punishment, there were in many prisons certain rituals involved when a condemned man was returned to await execution. At Armley Gaol a wooden chair was kept in the reception area, to be used exclusively by the condemned while awaiting transfer to their cells.

It was part of the prison folklore that no one other than the condemned ever sat in the chair and superstition had it that should someone other than a condemned prisoner do so, then he would be fated to hang.

In the spring of 1958 a number of prisoners had been seconded to help prison staff clean the reception area. Unaware of the 'curse', one of those detailed to help with the cleaning took the opportunity to rest his feet by sitting in the chair. He had been resting for several minutes when a guard came in and shouted for him to get up, telling him about the superstition.

The name of the convict was Ernest Raymond Jones.

13

A
FUGITIVE IN SLOW MOTION

The Murders of Joyce Moran and Neil Saxton at Rotherham,
April 1959

It was the evening of Tuesday 7th April 1959, and 33 year old physics lecturer Bernard Hugh Walden was part-way through teaching his class at Rotherham College of Technology when one of the pupils reminded him that he had promised to show them a past test-paper to help them prepare for the end of term exams. Walden told the class he would be gone a few minutes and left the room. He never returned. Moments later shots were heard in the corridor and two young people lay dying.

Detectives were at the scene within minutes. The two who had been shot were 20 year old Joyce Moran, a typist and clerk at the college, and her boyfriend, 21 year old Neil Saxton, a student at the college who lived with his parents in Sheffield.

Although no one had seen the actual shooting, Walden became the immediate suspect when it was found he had abandoned his class and when it became known that he had a crush on the pretty typist. Detectives, under the supervision of the Chief Constable of Rotherham CID, Mr James Cotton, released his name as the man they wished to interview in connection with the murder.

Amongst the first to the scene were Dr David Price, the county pathologist, and Rotherham police surgeon Dr Alan Smith. They found that Joyce, who had celebrated her 21st birthday just a few weeks earlier, had died instantly; her boyfriend died from his wounds shortly after reaching hospital.

Piecing together what had happened, it seemed that the lecturer had chanced upon the couple as he left the classroom to go to his locker.

Joyce Moran.

Seeing them laughing together, with Saxton leaning through the office window and Joyce sitting at her desk, had sent Walden into a jealous rage.

A keen shot, and a member of the local gun club, Walden kept a number of guns. These were kept both at his home, in his car boot, and despite a recent visit to the college by a member of the royal family, he also had one kept in his locker at work. It seemed that he had taken a Luger pistol out of his locker, gone towards the office and blasted Saxton once in the back before entering the room and pumping six bullets into Joyce. Examination showed that although the first bullet missed, Joyce had been shot in the chest as she made for the door, and a further four bullets were fired into her heart as she lay on the floor.

A manhunt was set up and notices were issued asking police throughout the country to be on the look-out for Walden, who was believed to be still armed and dangerous. A description of the killer was published in the press, depicting him as five feet seven inches tall, thinly built and walking with a distinctive limp. He was driving a blue Ford Prefect car with the registration plate SET 369, which on the following day was found abandoned in Leeds along with several pistols and ammunition; this was matched by ballistics experts to the cartridges found at the murder scene.

Piecing together what had caused the tragedy, police found that Walden had developed a crush on Joyce shortly after taking lodgings on Far Lane, Rotherham, the same street where the Moran family lived. Walden became friendly with Joyce's family and was a frequent visitor to their house, where from time to time he watched television. He also took both Joyce and the family for trips out in his motor car, and he often gave Joyce a lift into work before he moved to new lodgings across town at Spinneyfield.

It seemed that at some stage Walden had asked Joyce to marry him but she had laughed off the proposal. Two key incidents appeared to have triggered the murders. The first was Joyce Moran's 21st birthday in November 1958. Among the guests were both Bernard Walden and Neil Saxton, who had, unknown to Walden, been courting Joyce for a few months. Discovering that Joyce had a boyfriend was a body blow for the disabled lecturer who felt that it was his limp that had put Joyce off him.

The second incident occurred later at a college dance when she danced with Saxton brazenly in front of Walden, who told a colleague that if she ever made a fool of him again he would kill her.

Dr David Price examines the office at Rotherham College.

Bernard Walden was at liberty for several weeks and police investigations involved officers in forces around the country as well as Interpol. The nationwide hunt ended in the early hours of 1st May, when Police Constable Alan Hawkins spotted Walden sleeping in a park shelter in Reading, Berkshire. The man had a shotgun nestled against him and when asked what he was doing with it, Walden told the officer his name and said he was the man wanted for the murders in Rotherham. In the period leading up to his arrest Walden had travelled extensively across the country; one press report described him as 'a fugitive in slow motion', whose tell-tale limp prevented him from hurrying. He told detectives as he was driven back to Rotherham that after leaving his car in Leeds he had journeyed down to Leicester where he panicked when he thought he had been recognised by someone he knew and had then fled to London. He was in possession of a large sum of money at this point but as his travels took him to Torquay, Salisbury and Oxford where he had studied for his degree several years earlier, the money gradually dwindled away.

Walden's car found abandoned in Leeds.

From Oxford he had cycled to Reading where he was down to his last threepence when picked up by the police. In his possession was a shotgun which Walden claimed to have purchased whilst on the run with the intention of robbing a shop.

Mr Justice Paull presided over Walden's trial for capital murder at Sheffield Assizes at the end of June 1959. He pleaded not guilty. Mr George Waller QC told the court how two young people were found dying after shots were heard while lectures were in progress at the college on the evening of 7th April. Neil Saxton had been talking to Joyce Moran through the hatch at the office. On the following day Walden's car was found abandoned in Leeds and he was subsequently arrested, in possession of a shotgun, on 1st May.

Leading for the defence, Mr Henry Scott QC stated that the facts of the case would not be disputed and that the sole issue of the defence was Walden's mental state and the question of diminished responsibility. Mr Scott said that through contracting polio shortly after his mother's death whilst he was studying at Oxford, Walden had suffered two crushing disappointments. The first was that he had lost studies at a vital time and finished with a disappointing third-class degree, and the second that the disease had withered his leg, a matter of which he was deeply and bitterly conscious and rather ashamed.

Walden being returned to Rotherham.

'Walden believes he is a victim singled out by fate. He believes he has an absolute right to kill if he wishes,' Mr Scott told the court. Both his father, who had not seen his son for ten years, and Dr James Valentine, a psychiatrist from Ilkley mental hospital, gave evidence of abnormalities in his childhood that included sleepwalking and talking to himself.

Described by his colleagues at work as a brilliant scholar and a fine lecturer, Walden had become infatuated with Joyce Moran and out of jealousy because of her feelings for Saxton, had committed a brutal double murder.

Medical evidence called by the prosecution suggested that Walden did not show signs of any abnormality of the mind at the time and this was borne out by a statement he made regarding the murders and how he regretted his actions.

'I feel dreadful about causing these deaths – doing all that in the space of three seconds. If only I had the sense to count to ten it would have saved all this,' he said to Dr James Walker, the prison medical officer at Armley Gaol. He also alleged at one stage that he had planned to paralyse Saxton so that Joyce would leave him.

Evidence was introduced in court to show that Walden had a previous conviction for assaulting a 15 year old boy in 1948 with a poker. He had been bound over for 12 months for the offence and such was his shame he never saw his father again until his arrest for murder over ten years later.

When summing up the case, Mr Justice Paull asked Dr Valentine a vital question: whether Walden knew that what he was doing was wrong. The prisoner's fate was effectively sealed when the doctor replied that in his opinion, he did. On 1st July the trial ended when the jury of ten men and two women took just 15 minutes to find Walden guilty as charged. White-faced, he gripped the bars of the dock as sentence of death was passed on him.

His appeal, on the grounds that the trial judge had misdirected the jury in attempting to define mental abnormality, was heard at the end of July. The issue of diminished responsibility was discussed in further detail before the appeal was quickly dismissed by Lord Justice Hilbery. An application to appeal to the House of Lords was also declined and at 9 am on Friday 14th August 1959, Bernard Hugh Walden was hanged at Armley Gaol.

The timing of the murder was one of tragic coincidence. Both the killer and his male victim had recently taken up new jobs. Neil Saxton should not have been in Rotherham on that fateful night as he was due to go on a training course in Henley, but the course was put back a week and his appearance at the college had been a surprise for Joyce, whom he planned to take out for a drink when she finished work. Likewise, Walden had recently been offered a new post at Barnsley Technical College, but had decided to put off the position until his class had taken their exams.

14

THE
FATE OF FORTUNE

The Murder of Eli Myers at Leeds,
February 1961

The curtains at the house on Chel-
wood Avenue, in the Street Lane district of Leeds, had rarely been
opened in the 18 months that Eli Myers lived there. Known amongst his
fellow market traders as Jack Marsh, the 50 year old bachelor traded in
boys' and men's clothing and was well known on numerous market
stalls around Yorkshire. So long were the hours that he spent working
on the markets that he had little time at the house he had bought from
his sister in the summer of 1959. It was mainly used to store his goods
and as a place to sleep.

Fortune had smiled on Eli Myers one Saturday evening in December
1960, when along with a number of other marker traders and friends at
the Jewish Jubilee Hall at Chapeltown, he was part of a syndicate that
scooped over £15,000 on the football pools. The cheque came in the
following week, the money was divided out, and Eli Myers was richer
to the tune of £1,275. The windfall was a considerable sum in 1960 and
news of the syndicate's good fortune made the pages of the local
newspapers where it was read by one man in particular who was short
of money.

On the night of Friday 24th February 1961, Eli Myers returned home
from work to find that he had an intruder inside the kitchen at the back
of the house. The thief appeared to have ransacked his house,
presumably looking for money. A fight then ensued during which
Myers received facial injuries and cuts to his hand, seemingly the result
of struggling with someone carrying a knife. He then collapsed and
died.

Eli Myers failed to show up on the local market stall the next day. At 1.15 pm, his brother, Louis Myers, who had gone to the market to speak to him, called at the house and noticed that Eli's blue van was missing from outside. Louis thought it unlikely Eli had gone to work on another market and so it was with some trepidation that he approached the house. The front door was locked and when he tried to gain entry by the back door he saw that something was amiss.

Fragments of glass lay where someone had broken the French window, and lying on his back on the living-room floor was Eli Myers. The police were called and Chief Inspector Dixon took charge of inquiries.

It was clear from the injuries Myers had sustained that the police were investigating a murder, but it was only when pathologist Professor C. J. Polson carried out a post-mortem at Leeds University Hospital that the exact cause of death was established. It was later to be a key factor in the case.

While Polson was examining the body, detectives making inquiries in the area called at the house of Mrs Hilda Harris, the closest neighbour of Eli Myers. She told them that at 10 pm on the previous night she had heard sounds of a fierce quarrel. 'There was bad language, raised voices and sounds of a violent argument. It then ended suddenly,' she said. Asked what she had done about it, Mrs Harris told the bemused policemen that this type of quarrel was an everyday occurrence in these parts and she had thought nothing more of it.

Officers combing the city for any leads to the identity of the murderer soon found a number of clues in a deserted garage on the outskirts of the city. A passer-by had noticed bundles of new clothing abandoned on wasteland near the garage and investigations found that this was part of the clothing stolen from Eli Myers's van.

A further and more significant clue was left in the form of some second-hand and bloodstained clothing that had also been abandoned. Amongst the clothing was a jacket with a name written on the inside label. This led police to a house on Woodland Lane, in the Chapeltown district, where in the early hours of Sunday morning they spoke to Zsiga Pankotai.

Pankotai was a 31 year old Hungarian miner who lived not far from Myers, and when questioned by Chief Inspector Dixon he denied having anything to do with the murder. There was, however, other evidence linking the Hungarian to the crime in the form of traces of blood, of the same group as Myers's, found on the strap of his wristwatch, but more damning was a jacket found at Pankotai's house that was one of a new batch Myers had recently taken into stock. The jacket was identical to those in the van and it appeared that Pankotai had substituted his bloodstained jacket, found at the deserted garage, for a new one taken from the van.

On the following morning, Pankotai was arrested and brought before Mr Ralph Cleworth QC, the Leeds stipendiary magistrate, where he was charged with murdering Eli Myers and remanded in custody.

When Zsiga Pankotai stood before Mr Justice Ashworth at Leeds Assizes in April, he was charged with capital murder – murder in the furtherance of theft – a charge that if proven carried the death penalty.

Leading for the Crown, Mr Alastair Sharp QC said that the accused had stabbed and struck Eli Myers, probably with a heavy instrument such as a wooden chair, and that the victim had died as a result of his injuries. Pankotai had then ransacked the house looking for money, before stealing a quantity of clothing and Myers's van.

While there was little doubt that Pankotai had been in the house at the time Myers died, his counsel, Mr Henry Scott QC, tried to put forward a defence of manslaughter and called medical witnesses to support his claim that whilst the accused had been responsible for the man's death it was not a case of murder. He claimed that Myers had died from natural causes and cited evidence from Professor Polson that Myers had not died as a result of being stabbed or punched in the head.

Professor Polson's post-mortem had found that Myers had received cuts to his hand, presumably caused when fending off someone carrying a knife, and that he had been struck hard in the face which had resulted in a broken nose and displacement of his upper teeth. Death could have been from suffocation caused by blood from the nose and mouth filling the lungs, but Polson claimed that in his opinion Myers had died from shock, as the victim was also suffering from heart disease. 'In my opinion the injuries neither singly nor collectively were sufficient to have killed a healthy man, but in the presence of heart disease they caused his death,' Polson told the court.

Pankotai alleged in his defence that he had intended to scare Eli Myers when he picked up the bread-knife, after being caught in the house. Myers had then lunged at the accused in a struggle that was reported to have lasted for close on 30 minutes. He denied hitting him in the face with a chair as the Crown had claimed, but he did admit driving away in the victim's van, unaware if the victim was alive or dead.

ALL COMMUNICATIONS TO BE ADDRESSED TO
THE UNDER SHERIFF OF YORKSHIRE
(B. DODSWORTH)
TELEGRAMS: "GRADOD," YORK
TELEPHONES: 25503-3 YORK

LONDON AGENTS:—
BELL, BRODRICK & GRAY
THE RECTORY,
30, MARTIN LANE,
CANNON STREET, E.C.4.
TELEGRAMS: "BONDELLI,"
CANNON, LONDON
TELEPHONE: MANSION HOUSE
57-8 (5 LINES)

DUNCOMBE PLACE,
YORK.

19th. June 1961

Sir,

            Zsiga Pankotai

        I shall be glad if you will let me know if you will
able to undertake the execution of the above named
which has now been fixed for Thursday, June 29th. 1961.

        The execution will take place at Leeds Prison at
8 a. m.

                        Yours truly,

                        B C R. Wadsworth

                        Under Sheriff.

MR. H. B. Allen
Junction Hotel
Whitefield
Manchester

Letter sent to executioner, Harry Allen, requesting his services at the last hanging to take place at Leeds.

Closing for the defence, Mr Scott submitted that Pankotai was not guilty of murder if Myers died as a result of shock at finding him burgling his home.'The cause of Mr Myers's death relies entirely on the evidence of Professor Polson. If he said beyond peradventure that this death was due to blows Mr Myers received, there would have been no defence in this case. But, although his opinion is that death was probably a result of the blows, there is another possible cause of death and that death is due to the shock, quite apart from the blows.'

Summing up, Mr Justice Ashworth told the jury that when Pankotai struck Myers with the knife, if he intended or it could be inferred that he intended to cause grievous bodily harm, then in the law that was the malice aforethought required for the murder to be proven. The same situation would cover blows to Myers's head with the kitchen chair. However, the jury must be satisfied, beyond reasonable doubt, that the original injury was caused by a knife.

On 26th April Zsiga Pankotai was convicted of capital murder and sentenced to death. An appeal was launched on the basis that the trial judge had unfairly rejected the evidence of Professor Polson but this was dismissed as was the leave to appeal to the House of Lords.

On Thursday 29th June 1961, Zsiga Pankotai became the 93rd and last person hanged at Armley Gaol. The hangman was the country's last chief executioner, Harry Allen. In his diary Allen recorded that the Hungarian weighed 148 pounds; stood five feet six inches tall; and was given a drop of seven feet six inches.

15

A
MIDNIGHT SWIM

The Murder of Alfred Harland at Scarborough,
June 1965

Tuesday 22nd June 1965 was a pleasant summer's day and there had been a steady stream of customers soaking up the sun at North Bay swimming pool, an outdoor baths in the bustling holiday resort of Scarborough. The pool closed at tea-time and once the last of the visitors had departed, the two baths patrolmen, 23 year old David Chapman and 18 year old Richard Makinson, went to a local bar at the Scalby Mills Hotel.

Both Chapman and Makinson were new to their summer jobs. For Chapman in particular the job was most welcome, as he had been unemployed for a long time and had financial problems; he had started work only three weeks earlier. Despite being on duty on the following day, they stayed in the bar until after last orders, by which time both had consumed large amounts of beer and were clearly drunk as they shouted and sang their way to their homes in the town.

Their journey back took them past the North Bay swimming pool and both men then made the fateful decision to go for a midnight swim. It had been nothing more than an innocent suggestion and they planned to ask Alfred Harland, the 65 year old caretaker, to let them in for a quick dip.

Harland's duties meant he often worked well into the night during the holiday season, but despite their loud calls and knockings they were unable to attract his attention. They decided to scale the main gate and gain entry into the courtyard. The light in Harland's office was on, but looking through the window they saw it was deserted. Makinson told Chapman that the keys to the pool area were kept in this office and still keen on a moonlight dip, the pair decided to break into the office.

Chapman took the lead and smashed a window pane through which they both entered. They mistakenly assumed that Harland would be in the pool area, probably cleaning the changing room. It was at this point that they now realised that if caught on the premises, they could be in trouble. Chapman told Makinson to pull down a grille that partitioned the pool area from the changing-rooms. This would mean that if Harland heard the men splashing about he would be trapped in the changing area and unable to see who was trespassing.

It was after Makinson had closed the heavy grille door that Chapman turned his attention to the day's takings, which were also kept in Harland's office. It seems likely that up to this stage Chapman had intended only to break in for a swim, but because of his financial problems the temptation of the money became too much for him, in his drunken state, to resist.

As Chapman pondered over how to get at the money, Harland heard a noise from the pool area and Makinson rushed back to tell his friend that the caretaker, who had not as they had imagined been in the changing area, was on his way back to the office. Fearful at being apprehended, they decided to intercept Harland before he could reach the office.

Chapman entered the pool area unseen as the whole area was in total darkness, the only light coming from the elderly man's torch. He tried to hide behind the diving board, but was spotted by Harland when he made a noise. It is unclear exactly what actually took place next but the end result was that Harland ended up face down in the water.

His body was found early next morning. At 5 am the milk delivery arrived at the pool. The milkman sensed something amiss when he noticed the front door standing open. Cautiously, he made his way inside until he spotted the opened safe. The police were called and found Alf Harland floating in the pool; a murder inquiry was set up.

Despite their undoubted hangovers both patrolmen had arrived at work as normal and later that morning they were interviewed by detectives. Unsatisfied with their accounts, the police took them both into custody, where each made a statement about what had happened.

Makinson's account suggested that Chapman had deliberately pushed Harland into the pool with the intention of drowning him. They had then pulled the man's body from the water, removed his keys and gone back into the office, whereupon his friend had taken some money from the safe. What Makinson had done, as the police pointed out, was to accuse his friend of murder during the course of a robbery, a crime that if he was convicted, could be enough to send Chapman to the gallows.

Chapman's statement, however, suggested something quite different. According to his account, Chapman was beside the pool when Harland spotted him. The old man had then lunged at him, throwing a punch, a movement that caused Harland to lose his balance, and as he fell into the pool he knocked his head against the base of the diving board.

Harland's semi-conscious body came to the surface of the pool. 'I saw his arms move. He was struggling for a second. I didn't know whether he could swim. He seemed to go limp in the water,' Chapman told detectives, claiming he had panicked because the events were happening too quickly for him to help.

However, the officers interviewing Chapman noticed the coldness with which he admitted that he knew that if he rescued Harland he would be arrested for breaking and entering and for robbing the takings from the office. To help himself to escape, Chapman said, he had pushed the body away as it floated near him.

Moments later, Makinson arrived beside the pool and realising what they were doing was wrong, together they fished him out of the water. Chapman told how they had then tried to save the old man: 'We put him on the side of the pool on his back. I tried to feel a pulse and there wasn't one. I put my hand close to his mouth to see if he was breathing and I couldn't detect any breath. I didn't see his chest moving. I didn't see any white froth coming from his mouth. I thought he was dead.'

Continuing, Chapman described the robbery: 'We went back to the office. Makinson opened the safe with the key. There were three cash bags. I opened one and passed one to Makinson, which he opened. I opened a third and Makinson went out.'

Chapman concluded his account by claiming that Makinson had gone back to the pool and on his return said that he had dumped the old man back in the water. Giggling drunkenly, Makinson had told him: 'I've put Alf back!'

While the two men were being interviewed at the police station Home Office pathologist Dr D. Hainsworth, who had arrived earlier that morning from Leeds University, carried out a post-mortem. He noted that as the body had been removed from the water a copious amount of white foam had come out of the nose and mouth. Dr Hainsworth found cuts and bruises on the man's scalp, but they were not serious. He stated that the blows were struck from above. There was a bruise above the right eye. He concluded his report by stating that the cause of death was drowning, adding that Harland was in poor health: he had already had a heart-attack and the doctor believed he could have suffered another at any time.

The atmosphere at the packed Leeds courtroom was solemn when in October the pair appeared at the Yorkshire Assizes before Mr Justice Havers. Together they were charged with capital murder. Both men had pleaded not guilty to the murder charge, but guilty to charges of breaking and entering and the theft of over £50.

The case for the prosecution as outlined by Mr John Cobb QC was that Chapman had struck Alfred Harland repeatedly near the pool and then pushed him away when the old man desperately tried to escape; afterwards Makinson, realising that the old man was alive, threw him back in the pool, knowing this would almost certainly kill him. Mr Cobb submitted that both men had had a hand in the old man's death and therefore both were equally guilty of capital murder.

Mr Peter Stanley-Price QC, defending Chapman, asked his client: 'Did you push him at all?'

The emphatic reply was: 'No, sir.'

Makinson was defended by Mr Rudolph Lyons QC. On the third day of the trial he called his client into the witness box: 'Did you kill Alfred Harland?'

'No, sir,' Makinson replied.

Mr Lyons probed further: 'Did you play any part in his death?'

Again the same answer.

Makinson then told the court he had no criminal record and had worked at the pool for six months. He had a good work record and liked Alfred Harland. He admitted drinking between six and nine pints of beer that night and that he was drunk. He denied there was any premeditated design to break in for the purpose of robbery and said that they just wanted a swim.

He told the court that when Chapman instructed him to pull down the grille, he thought it was to be a practical joke on the old man. The pulling-down of the grille made so much noise that Harland came running towards him. Makinson then said to Chapman: 'Let's get out and come back later.'

Makinson claimed he escaped and once in the street he looked back and saw Harland peering over a wall. 'I saw Dave was speaking to Harland . . . I did not think anything wrong was going on.'

Then, damning his erstwhile friend, he said he could see Chapman on the diving board pushing Harland back into the water as the old man struggled to the surface. He told the court that he told Chapman to stop: 'Pack it in . . . what the hell did you do that for?'

Chapman was alleged to have said: 'Shut up. We've got what we came for.'

This last statement was crucial, since according to Chapman's statement, the pair had up to this point not stolen the takings. Makinson also alleged that Chapman had then looked coldly at him and said: 'I had to do it – he recognised me.'

Finishing his evidence, Makinson claimed he had only helped to throw Harland's body back into the pool out of fear of Chapman.

Cross-examined by Mr Stanley-Price, Makinson was asked why he shared the proceeds of robbery. 'I don't know. We just agreed to split it,' he said quietly.

Counsel continued by pointing out that although Makinson claimed he had seen Chapman pushing a drowning man back into the water, he was an accomplice and very drunk and the court must not rely too much on this evidence. He also pointed out that the robbery was not preconceived.

Making the final speech for the Crown, Mr Cobb said that there could be no doubt that this was a grave and dreadful case, 'reflecting a degree of callousness and brutality the like of which one would fail to believe would be within the capacity of a human being'. He conceded that Makinson was a man of previous good character but that he had indirectly at least participated in the night's violence and had been quite content to share the cash. On the question of drunkenness, Mr Cobb said firmly: 'Drink is no defence . . . I would ask you to consider whether he is not using drink as something of a shield.'

In his summing-up, Mr Justice Havers said first, with reference to Makinson, that there was no criminal offence in failing to help a drowning man. Addressing the jury, he then said: 'Where there is a conflict of testimony between one or more of the witnesses for the prosecution . . . or defence, it is for you [the jury] to decide which you accept.'

Finally, the judge posed the question of whether the men were working in concert or whether one them could have genuinely not known that the other intended murder.

The jury retired for two and a half hours before returning to deliver a verdict. They found Chapman guilty of capital murder, while in the case of Makinson they found him not guilty of either murder or manslaughter. Makinson was, however, found guilty of being an accessory after the fact of grievous bodily harm.

There was a deathly hush in the court as the black cap was draped upon the head of the judge. Addressing the prisoner, Mr Justice Havers told Chapman: 'The jury, upon abundant evidence, have found you guilty of a callous and brutal murder . . . The sentence of the court upon you is that you suffer death in the manner authorised by law.'

Richard Makinson was put on probation for two years. Outside the court Chapman's wife, Margaret, burst into tears as she learnt of the jury's verdict. During the trial it had emerged that Chapman had a criminal record for acts of violence: in November 1959 he had been convicted of actual bodily assault, and in May 1962 he had been sent to Borstal for a similar offence.

Although Chapman did not appeal against his conviction, on 9th November he was formally reprieved when the Murder (Abolition of the Death Penalty) Act received royal assent; his sentence was changed to one of life imprisonment.

David Stephen Chapman, the Scarborough swimming baths murderer, has a place in the annals of criminal history as the last man in Great Britain to be sentenced to death for murder.

16

KILLER
ON THE LOOSE

The Murders of Police Constable David Haigh at Harrogate,
George Luckett at Girton,
and Police Sergeant David Winter at Malton,
June 1982

Police Constable David Haigh had been on duty for just an hour and a half on the morning of Thursday 17th June 1982, when he spotted the green Citroën motor car parked on the outskirts of Knaresborough Forest, close to Harrogate. Twenty-nine year old Haigh, who lived with his wife and three young sons in Elmwood Street, Harrogate, approached the car and spoke to the driver.

Asked to show some identification, the driver said he wasn't carrying anything but gave his name as Clive Jones and his date of birth as 18th October 1944. Noticing that the man had been sleeping rough, Haigh also thought he bore a resemblance to a man police wished to speak to in connection with an assault in a Harrogate public house in January. It was when he told 'Mr Jones' that he was taking him into custody pending further inquiries that the man suddenly whipped out a .22 Beretta automatic pistol and at point-blank range blasted the officer through the head, before speeding off. Although mortally wounded, the officer managed to write the Citroën's registration number in his notebook.

PC Haigh's body was found a short time later when, after he had failed to respond to a number of radio messages, a patrol car was dispatched to find out what had happened.

A manhunt for the killer of PC Haigh was set up under the guidance

Barry Peter Prudom.

of Mr David Burke, Assistant Chief Constable of North Yorkshire. Two clues led detectives to Barry Peter Prudom, also known as Barry Peter Edwards, a 37 year old electrician from Leeds. Prudom was the man police wished to speak to in connection with the assault in January and the warrant for his arrest carried his date of birth as 18th October 1944.

A sharp-eyed officer noticed the same date when furnished with the information police had obtained from Haigh's notebook. The second and decisive link was when the registration number of the green Citroën was found to belong to Prudom. The car was found on the following day and fingerprints matched those of Prudom. The search for the killer had begun.

Prudom, known to be an ex-SAS reservist, trained in survival and a crack shot, laid low for most of the following week until he turned up at a house in Girton, near Newark in Nottinghamshire. On Wednesday 23rd June, hungry and tired, Prudom broke into a house owned by 52 year old George Luckett who lived with his wife Sylvia on a smallholding. Prudom tied the couple together and after eating some food he went into the garage to have a look at their motor car and see if it had fuel.

Returning to the house, Prudom saw that Luckett had freed himself and was standing in the kitchen holding a shotgun. He then crept back inside, disarmed the occupant, and shot him dead with his own gun. Before fleeing the house he callously shot Sylvia Luckett in the head. She survived the attack but was left crippled and brain damaged.

Officers investigating the murder at Girton liaised with Detective Superintendent John Carlton who was handling the murder of PC Haigh, as it was believed that Prudom had shot both men and the woman. He was also now known to be driving the Lucketts' brown Rover car.

Prudom returned to Yorkshire with the intention of lying low in Dalby Forest but on the following day he stumbled across officers searching the moorland. PC Kenneth Oliver, a dog handler, was shot at by Prudom. Fortunately, although seven shots were fired at him, Prudom's aim was off and he received only minor wounds.

The next officers to come into contact with the fugitive were not so fortunate. Despite an intensive search of the area, Prudom was still at liberty; he ventured out of hiding and purchased some food at Wood's general store at Old Malton. As he walked back to his hiding place he was spotted by two police officers on duty stopping and questioning motorists on the A64 on the outskirts of Malton.

Sergeant David Winter and PC Michael Woods noticed the man, and Winter approached. Sensing something was about to happen, Woods cried out 'Watch it, Dave', but it was too late. Prudom pulled out his Beretta and pointed it at the officer. Winter fled with Prudom in pursuit. The sergeant tried to climb a wall to make good his escape but Prudom closed in and fired three times, the last shot as Winter lay in a heap on the ground.

Prudom made off across fields as PC Woods summoned help. Police, who had been searching the area a few miles away, hurried to Malton and residents were told to keep indoors as armed officers combed the town for the triple killer. Locals making their way home from town dived for cover at one point when shots were fired at a television crew covering the story. The area took on the appearance of a war zone, as helicopters swooped low overhead and scores of heavily armed men prowled the area.

With over 800 officers involved in the manhunt, Chief Constable Kenneth Henshaw then played his ace card. He recruited a survival expert, 46 year old ex-SAS man Eddie McGee, who ran a survival centre at Pateley Bridge. McGee was the author of a book entitled *No Need to Die: Real Techniques of Survival*, with which Prudom was known to be familiar.

With McGee's assistance, officers soon found where the killer had been hiding out. A 'hide' measuring six feet by three feet was found in a Forestry Commission fir plantation near Cawthorne. As the search area was narrowed down, the number of officers on the case was likewise scaled down.

A plea by Carol Francis, Prudom's girlfriend of four years, to surrender was reported in the press after police had said that they would shoot to kill if necessary. It brought no response. Senior detectives thought that the killer might have taken hostages in a remote house and this was indeed the case.

On Saturday evening, 3rd July, Prudom approached a house on East Mount, Malton, less than 300 yards from the local police station. After hiding in an out-building for a short time he entered and took an elderly couple hostage. Maurice and Bessie Johnson were alone in the house when Prudom came in. Mrs Johnson spotted him first.

'You know who I am, don't you?' Prudom said, pointing the gun that had so far killed two police officers and a civilian.

'I'm sorry, I don't,' Mrs Johnson replied calmly. Seeing that she was making no attempt to create a scene, Prudom led her into the front room, where her husband had been watching television. He bound the couple together before cooking himself bacon and eggs. Seeing the old couple were in some discomfort with their bindings, Prudom showed the other side of his nature by helping them become comfortable.

As the killer talked to his captors, their son returned home. Fortunately, he too didn't put up a struggle, an action that undoubtedly saved his life. Forty-three year old Brian Johnson was tied up but Prudom, after assurances that there wouldn't be any trouble, freed the parents and made them a cup of tea.

Prudom told his hostages of the events that had led him to their home. A bond seemed to develop between killer and hostage and after he had made a full confession, the family tried to persuade him to give himself up.

'No. I'll never let the police take me. I'll kill myself first,' Prudom said, adding that if he went this way he would take as many police with him as he could. He then asked for something to eat, calling it his last supper. It was clear that Prudom had reached the end of the road: he had become mentally tired and physically exhausted, and his feet were so blistered he could hardly walk.

In the early hours of Sunday morning, Prudom slipped from the house. Two hours later his captors were able to free themselves and call the police. The manhunt began to close in on Barry Prudom.

A posse of police including 12 heavily armed officers, led by Chief Inspector David Clarkeson and including survival expert Eddie McGee, arrived at the house. McGee noticed some footprints in the morning dew and followed the trail to Malton Tennis Club, less than 100 yards away. Crawling on his stomach he inched across the ground until he came across a lean-to shelter. He pulled at some plastic sheeting covered in brambles and noticed a human foot. He had found the fugitive.

Without making a sound, McGee returned to where the officers had grouped and told them what he had found. It was still uncertain at this point that they had found Prudom; perhaps it was a tramp sleeping rough. The only way was for the officers to approach and confront the man.

Clarkeson closed in and pushed at the shelter. Prudom responded by letting off a volley of shots. Clarkeson fled to safety, from where he called for the killer to surrender. Prudom answered with further shots, at which point the police chief gave orders for his men to open fire. In what was later described as like a scene from *Starsky and Hutch*, the shoot-out went on for several minutes.

During the shoot-out police had thrown two stun grenades but they failed to have the desired effect, nor was it possible to use CS gas as the wind was blowing in the wrong direction. The police stopped firing and waited. Nothing. Clarkeson picked up one of the heavy shields and advanced. As he approached the shelter he saw Prudom, lying on the ground clutching his gun. The 17-day manhunt was over.

At the inquest held in Scarborough, it was found that Prudom had taken his own life: he had shot himself in the head. At the subsequent inquiry, information about Prudom's background was revealed which gave some indication of why he embarked on the series of crimes which led to one of the largest-ever manhunts in the region.

In 1969 Prudom had served in the Territorial SAS at Leeds, as a reservist, but had failed to earn a place as a regular volunteer. He had not let this disappointment unduly upset him and became a stable, hard-working man. In 1977 he bought an off-licence for his wife Gillian, but finding his income could not support their lifestyle, he opted to go out to Saudi Arabia to work as a contract electrician.

It was while here, working hard and sending money home, that he was devastated to receive a 'Dear John' letter from his wife. Not only had she taken up with another man but when he returned to Leeds he found that she had cleared nearly £8,000 from their account.

From then on he became morose and irritable and this culminated in an incident in a public house when he assaulted a man. A few months earlier he had returned from a holiday in America where he purchased a pistol, which he managed to smuggle back into the country. It was the same Beretta pistol that he would use to kill two serving police officers and with which he would take his own life.

There was uproar at Malton shortly after the death of Barry Prudom when his girlfriend refused to pay for his funeral. It was reported that the costs would have to be met by the local council and when it was announced that he would be given a pauper's burial in a plot adjacent to Sergeant Winter, one of his victims, there was national outrage. Fortunately the situation was defused when a relative came forward with the money and Prudom was buried at a private family service.

The leading officers involved in the manhunt, along with the families of the murdered officers, were awarded commendations, as was Eddie McGee. Asked about his part in the investigation McGee was modest about his help, but made a fitting quip when asked by a reporter if Prudom had learned his lessons well from the book. 'It's not much of a bloody lesson if he's in a box,' McGee replied laconically.

17

THE
DANGERS OF DEBT

The Murder of Ivy Preston at Bradford,
September 1985

There is a famous saying that greed accounts for most of man's dishonesty. Greed, one of the seven deadly sins, is also one of the classic motives for murder, as this sad case from Bradford in the mid-1980s bears out.

Detectives investigating the brutal murder of Ivy Preston were baffled at the savagery of the beating. It was on Sunday morning, 29th September 1985, that the silver-haired 75 year old spinster was found battered and strangled behind the living room door at her house at Burdale Place, Listerhills, Bradford, and to the experienced officers called to the scene, something wasn't right.

The victim's clothes had been rearranged as if to suggest that a sexual assault had taken place but even a cursory examination revealed that this was not the case. Nothing appeared to have been taken from the house, and also baffling to detectives was the extent of the injuries: it was as if someone had attacked with a real hatred. Blood was liberally spattered across the living room, and the killer had rolled up the fireside rug and placed it under the sofa.

A search of the house uncovered close on £1,000 in buff-coloured wage packets, many dating back to pre-decimalisation days. Neighbours who knew the victim gave police some background information on the unfortunate woman.

Ivy Preston had a mistrust of banks and her frugality was well known. She had never married – her fiancé had been tragically killed many years earlier, and she had worked all her life in the local textile mills. In 1965, ten years before she retired, Ivy had purchased her terraced house. The sale had been a local talking-point for weeks after; Ivy had paid cash for the property, but not in notes. Instead, she had produced a suitcase full of sixpences and half-crowns, and it had taken close on four hours to count out the money.

All in all, it seemed that someone had killed the old lady in an attempt to steal her money. It was left up to Detective Chief Superintendent Kenneth Cooper and his team to find those responsible.

Among friends, neighbours and relatives routinely questioned on the following day was Ivy's great-niece 19 year old Allyson Kirk, a clerk at the Yorkshire Building Society in Bradford, who lived with her 21 year old husband Ian in Carr Road, Todmorden. They had become quite close to the old lady in recent months, having taken her on holiday in the summer, and they were known to have visited 'Aunt Ivy' on the Saturday she died.

The young couple seemed genuinely shocked at the news of her death, in particular Allyson, who seemed so distraught that a policewoman made her a cup of tea as she sobbed her heart out in the lounge. Ian Kirk told Detective Inspector Eddie Hemsley that he had dropped Allyson off at Ivy's house whilst he drove to a car-wash, and after returning to pick up his wife, they had left Aunt Ivy in good health at around 6.30 pm.

A few discreet inquiries showed that the young couple were heavily in debt. The knowledge that Ivy was thought to be well off, and that she had been robbed, made them suspects until they could prove otherwise.

Hemsley pondered over the couple for 24 hours and decided on a hunch to return to Todmorden to ask further questions. He found the house empty when he called but rather than return to Bradford, he decided to poke around for clues. The detective struck lucky almost at once. Lifting the dustbin lid in the back yard, he found a tee-shirt that had been recently washed but still bore a faint staining. More importantly, he noticed shreds of buff-coloured paper which he thought looked similar to the old wage packets that had been found at Ivy's house.

Hemsley radioed through his discovery and a search for the Kirks was orchestrated. Within the hour they were picked up and in their car was found close on £1,500 in another of those buff-coloured envelopes, inside the glove compartment.

The young couple were taken to Bradford police station where, after an initial denial, they each broke down and confessed. In an attempt to

Burdale Place, Bradford, where Ivy Preston lived.

save their own skins they at once tried to throw one another to the wolves by each blaming the other for the murder. Satisfied that both were to blame, police charged them together with the murder.

Mr Justice Kennedy presided over the seven-day trial at Leeds Crown Court in the summer of 1987. Mr Martin Bethel QC led for the Crown and described how the pair had selected their victim for 'a perfect murder'. The court heard a tale of foolishness and greed, and it was shown how easily a young, newly married couple could find themselves in debt.

Ian Kirk and Allyson Northin had been childhood sweethearts. On her 17th birthday they became engaged and shortly afterwards she left home after a quarrel and moved in with Ian and his family in Todmorden. Allyson had been a bright girl, and after leaving school with a number of 'O' levels she first went to work in a post office before finding a good job at the Yorkshire Building Society. By contrast, Ian left school without qualifications but managed to find manual work with a local firm.

Early in 1985, they were married and amongst the guests was Allyson's great-aunt, Ivy Preston. Within months of getting married the Kirks found themselves heavily in debt. It was easy to obtain finance from the credit companies, but they soon found that although spending was great fun, the repayments were an altogether different matter.

By the summer they were in debt to the tune of £8,000. The sorry state of their finances made grim reading. They still owed money for the legal fees on the house; they were overdrawn at three banks; in debt to five loan companies for such luxuries as a new car, furniture and a bathroom suite; and they owed money on two credit cards and to three mail-order companies. Then there were hire purchase payments on their television, video recorder and hi-fi, as well as outstanding bills owed for gas, electricity and telephone. Added to this were various sums of money lent by members of the family – including a £200 loan from Aunt Ivy. The whole picture was one of dire financial straits.

Quite when the Kirks picked on Allyson's aunt as a solution to their financial problems is uncertain, but they did become more friendly with the old lady as their debts mounted. So much so, that they even invited her to spend a week's caravanning holiday with them at Filey. Ivy was pleased to accept, but even then she had to find the money to fund the trip.

It was during this trip, Mr Bethel alleged, that Ian Kirk left his wife and her great-aunt in Filey and travelled back alone to her house in Bradford where he unsuccessfully tried to break in. It was on his return, the Crown alleged, that they decided that Aunt Ivy should die.

The cold, calculated method in which they had planned the murder shocked those who heard it outlined in court. Allyson chose to carry out the killing and it was decided that she would do this by strangling the old lady with a ligature made from a blanket. Fearing that she might lack the strength both of body and mind to carry out the murder this way, Ian suggested that she use a hammer to batter Aunt Ivy over the head. Finding this an easier alternative, Allyson practised her technique, encouraged by her husband, by striking the hammer on the floor. On the evening of the murder, with her hammer secreted inside her knitting bag, Allyson called at the house.

When Ian Kirk took the stand in the witness box, he denied knowing that his wife planned to commit murder when he dropped her off at her aunt's huse. 'I never murdered anyone,' he told the court, 'it was my wife.' Under cross-examination, Kirk did admit that after the old lady had been murdered he had driven Allyson up to Morecambe Bay where they had thrown away the hammer. His counsel pleaded that Ian Kirk was at most guilty of being an accessory after the fact to murder.

The trial ended with verdicts of guilty in both cases and they were each sentenced to life imprisonment. Turning first to Allyson, Mr Justice Kennedy told her: 'You have listened, as I have listened, to the account of what you did to a woman for whom it is said you have an affection. The offence is inexplicable.' He then passed sentence on her, before turning to her husband and giving out the same sentence.

Kenneth Cooper, head of Bradford CID, the detective who had led the murder inquiry, later described the case as a lesson in bad housekeeping and related how two perfectly respectable and ordinary people let their financial affairs get so out of hand that the intense pressure drove them to plan in cold blood and commit a murder of the most brutal nature.

$\boxed{18}$

LICENSED
TO KILL

The Murders of Danielle Lloyd and Stephanie Lloyd
at Stannington,
September 1986

There was high drama at Amiens Cathedral, in northern France, as an angry crowd shouted abuse at the Englishman perched 200 feet above them who was clinging precariously to a stone gargoyle. 'Jump,' they cried, as Superintendent Robert Canonge, chief of the French police, tried patiently to talk him down.

It was on the afternoon of Thursday 28th October 1986 that the man, who had been on a tour of the imposing cathedral, handed a note to the guide before vaulting a parapet and threatening to jump. The note read 'I am psychologically depressed. Please call a priest.'

Soon there was a large crowd gathered at the foot of the building, including a television crew who filmed the incident for both the local and later worldwide news. The man was revealed to be a 37 year old Sheffield solicitor, Ian Wood, wanted in his own country for the murder of his mistress, 38 year old Danielle Lloyd, a native of Amiens, and her young daughter Stephanie.

Wood clung to the stone figure as the police chief was joined below by the town's mayor, a local priest, and a number of gendarmes, who tried to coax him down. After six hours, and with Wood's concentration wavering, one of the gendarmes was able to grab him and after a brief struggle he reluctantly allowed himself to be brought down and placed under arrest. As he was taken to the local police station, the angry mob kicked at the car, shouting 'English bastard'. Asked why he hadn't

Ian Wood perched high up on Amiens Cathedral.

Mrs Danielle Lloyd and her two children.

jumped, Wood said that with the crowd howling for him to do so, he didn't want to give them the satisfaction, as it would be like 'the last act of a sad circus clown'.

On the following day extradition papers were prepared so that Wood could be brought back to stand trial for the murders which just over a month earlier had shocked the quiet community of Stannington, a picturesque village standing high on the moors on the outskirts of Sheffield.

A murder inquiry had been set up at the end of September when Danielle Lloyd and her two children, three year old Stephanie and five year old Christopher, were found to have been shot at Ughill Hall, the spacious mansion that Wood shared with his French-born mistress. Relatives concerned for the children's welfare had called the police and officers had broken into the Hall. All three had been shot in the head and although both mother and daughter had died from their injuries, amazingly the young lad survived the attack and was later to make almost a full recovery.

Detective Chief Superintendent Robin Herold was put in charge of the case and looking into the background of Wood, he found he had led a fascinating life. Wood was the son of the wealthy director of a Sheffield steel works, and was educated privately at the expensive Haileybury public school. He chose a career in law and after graduating from Sheffield University with a third-class honours degree in 1968 Wood found a position in a local legal firm.

In 1975 he set up his own successful practice and in the following year married Margaret, an English girl he had met whilst holidaying in France. In the course of the next decade as his family grew to include a daughter and three sons, his business also prospered. Wood was appointed clerk to the city's tax commissioners, a post which brought a hefty salary that allowed the family to take over Ughill Hall, an 18-bedroom mansion at Stannington.

Ian Wood had been married for ten years when he first met Danielle Lloyd. Born Danielle Ledez in Amiens, she had moved to England in 1975 where she met and married a Sheffield schoolteacher, Colin Lloyd. Lloyd was her second husband, her first having died in a flying accident three years earlier.

Wood became infatuated with the French beauty when she called at his office in the autumn of 1985 and asked him to begin divorce proceedings against her husband. He began to shower her with expensive gifts and when she returned his feelings he left his wife and family and set up home with Danielle. His estranged wife was left at Ughill Hall, but unable to afford to run a house of that size without her husband's salary she was forced to leave; in January 1986, Wood moved his mistress and her two children into the Hall.

There were a number of other important things the police discovered as they made a dossier on Ian Wood. First, his business was now in such a bad state that he had been swindling customers out of vast sums of money in order to finance a lifestyle beyond his means, and second,

Danielle was pregnant with his child. They also found that despite leaving his wife for Danielle, Wood had also installed another mistress in a Sheffield hotel.

With the mother and daughter in the local mortuary, and her son in intensive care at the Royal Hallamshire Hospital, Detective Chief Superintendent Herold began a hunt for the killer. It was discovered that Wood had hired a car, and police officers in Yorkshire as well as customs officers at ports throughout the country were asked to be on the look-out for a Ford Granada Scorpio, with the registration number C832 AMS.

On Tuesday 23rd September, three days after the murder, events took a dramatic turn when Wood telephoned a reporter on the local *Sheffield Gazette*. He confessed that he had killed his mistress and her daughter but claimed it was part of a suicide pact. Danielle, he claimed, was going through a difficult time with her impending divorce and as her husband was making more and more demands, she had reached breaking point. 'I know it was a most appalling thing, but I must keep my side of the bargain,' he said before ringing off.

Wood also insisted that the suicide pact had certain conditions to which he must adhere before finishing his side of the bargain. First, he was to see that Danielle was buried in her home town and that her husband did not attend the funeral. Wood told the reporter that if these 'conditions' weren't met, he would kill Colin Lloyd.

In the following weeks Wood was to make dozens of calls to the same reporter and although detectives tried to trace them, they were unsuccessful. It was still believed, however, that Wood was in the Yorkshire area, and detectives were no nearer bringing the fugitive to justice when they heard from their French counterparts that the killer had been apprehended in Amiens.

Returned to face justice in his own country, Ian Wood's trial opened at Sheffield Crown Court on Wednesday 22nd July 1987. He pleaded guilty to the murder of three year old Stephanie, but admitted only manslaughter in the case of his mistress. He was also charged with the attempted murder of Christopher Lloyd and a number of theft charges.

Opening for the Crown, Mr Geoffrey Rivlin QC said that he planned to reject the manslaughter plea and pursue a conviction of murder on both counts. Rivlin told the court of the events leading up to the murders. On that Sunday morning, 21st September, Wood had finally confessed to Danielle that he had stolen large sums of money from clients. It was alleged that they then made love, after which Wood said that he would go to the police on the following morning.

Suddenly, without warning, Wood crept up behind his mistress, and using a cushion to muffle the explosion, shot her twice with an Enfield army pistol. With grim coincidence, it was the very same pistol that his father had used to commit suicide some time before. He then entered Stephanie's room, telling her he wanted to play a game of hide-and-seek. Covering her face with a duvet, he shot her twice in the head. Wood then went into Christopher's room and tried to repeat the cold-blooded execution. Astonishingly, the youngster managed to survive the attack. For almost 24 hours he had lain in the bathroom, his skull shattered from the shooting.

The prosecution said they planned to show that Wood's claim of a suicide pact was nothing but a carefully thought out lie. By implying her death was part of a suicide pact – 'a suicide tryst' Wood had called it – he felt he had grounds for a defence of manslaughter. As children cannot by law comply to a suicide pact, Wood, with his legal background, knew he had to face a murder charge in respect of Stephanie.

Wood took the stand on the fourth day of the trial and said that he and Danielle had discussed committing suicide. They had planned to take a drug overdose but as it would have been difficult to get the children to take tablets, he had opted to shoot them instead. Speaking in his defence, Wood's mother said that she was aware that Danielle had made a number of threats to end her own life, and those of her children, claiming that she had said 'there is no joy in living in the constant fear of Colin'.

Summing up the trial on the seventh day, Rivlin said that Wood was 'an utterly ruthless and cold-blooded killer' and dismissed the suicide pact as 'a pack of lies'. He told the court that if the situation was not so desperately serious it would be laughable: 'Wood is a man with an unusually fertile imagination when it seems convenient, and it has served him well in different circumstances . . . this man has the capacity to dream up an extraordinary tissue of lies when it suits his purpose. Call it lies or romancing, it all comes very easy to him,' he said in the conclusion to his address.

Wood's counsel, in closing his case, restated his client's defence of a suicide pact with Mrs Lloyd. He asked the jury what benefit Wood could derive from lying after pleading guilty to one murder and not the other. 'Was it sadistic pleasure? No, this was a suicide pact, and into this pact two normal, rational people had pooled their tension, their stresses and extraordinary personalities, and came out with the most calamitous of all schemes.'

Trial judge Mr Justice Taylor urged the jury not to be swayed by feelings of revulsion. 'What you have heard in this case must create horror and perhaps indignation in the minds of most reasonable people. Wood must prove that it is more probable than not that he and Danielle agreed that both of them die, and it is more probable than not that when he killed Danielle he had settled a firm intention of dying himself in pursuance of the agreement.'

The jury, rejecting his story, found Wood guilty by majority verdict on both counts. Passing sentence, the judge told him: 'I have no doubt you were under great pressure at the time but these were cold-blooded shootings of your mistress and her daughter and son, and you were prepared to kill all three of them. Having shot them you packed methodically, dressed smartly, had a drink in your favourite bar and set off for France in a hire car for which the police would not be looking. You then tried to put a better complexion on things by sending back a stream of messages saying Danielle had agreed to do it. You stuck to this tale throughout the long and anguished trial.'

He then sentenced Wood to two life sentences for the murder of Mrs Lloyd and her daughter, and 12 years' imprisonment for the attempted murder of her son. Wood also received three years on charges relating to theft from clients. All sentences were to run concurrently.

It was revealed at the end of the trial that the murder weapon, an ex-service Enfield revolver, had been returned to Wood by the Sussex police after the suicide of his father. This had been at Wood's request, even though at the time he did not have the necessary licence and had not notified the local police.

Police had later been called to interview Wood after he had become involved in a fierce argument with staff at a Sheffield gunshop when he was sold the wrong size ammunition by mistake. His attitude was such that the shop manager contacted the police, warning that in his opinion Wood's temper made him an unfit person to possess a firearm. Police had once before confiscated his gun following a domestic row in 1985, only for it to be returned later.

Following the incident in the gunshop, inquiries were made and the matter was dealt with. It was surprising, then, that a short time later, when Wood's licence came up for renewal, the authorities found it in themselves to grant another licence – a licence to kill.

ACKNOWLEDGEMENTS

I would like to thank the following people for their help towards compiling *Yorkshire Murder Casebook*. Special thanks go to both Tim Leech and Matthew Spicer who kindly loaned me cuttings, photographs and other archive materials from their own collections, and also to Lisa Moore who helped me through all stages of the book.

Thanks also to Margot Armitidge at Crookes Books, Sheffield, who kindly loaned me books from her personal collection.

I would like to thank staff in the libraries and record offices at Bolton, Manchester, Pontefract, Darlington, Dewsbury, Leeds, Huddersfield, Rotherham, Bradford and Scarborough.

For help with photos I would like to thank Adrian Greenhalgh at the Bolton Institute.

We have tried to trace the copyright owners on all pictures and apologise if we have inadvertently contravened any existing copyrights.

Finally my thanks go once again to Nicholas and Suzanne Battle, and Paula Leigh at Countryside Books for helping me put together this my fourth book in the Murder Casebook series.

INDEX